Praise for *The Young Athlete's Guide to Playing Sports*

"As an intercollegiate athletic director at Colgate and Northwestern for over 16 years, I saw first-hand many of the problems associated with youth sports, including over involved parents and entitled athletes. Jeff Rhoads has written a book that will be a big help in improving youth sports. Jeff focuses on the benefits the athlete gains through participation, not the long shot chances of an athlete earning a scholarship or becoming a professional. Jeff and I grew up together (outside of Buffalo) playing pick-up basketball games, and I know that he fully understands the benefits of youth sports done the right way. "

–Mark H. Murphy,
President & CEO,
GREEN BAY PACKERS

"In the Young Athlete's Guide to Playing Sports, Jeff does a wonderful job guiding the young athlete, youth coaches and parents through a wide range of training drills, positive mental concepts and life experiences. Most importantly, he captures the essential balance of fun and learning for all."

–Dave Littlefield,
General Manager 2001-2007,
PITTSBURGH PIRATES

"The Young Athlete's Guide to Playing Sports offers an excellent introduction for kids who want to play a sport or for the player already on the team who wants to get better. The Guide is also a must read for parents and coaches as it outlines the balance required to help young athletes build a healthy, fun, and successful sports experience."

–David Stevenson,
President & CEO,
CENTRAL CONNECTICUT COAST YMCA

"As an Athletic Director, basketball coach, and parent, I found Jeff's book refreshing and a must read for young athletes, parents and coaches. Jeff identifies that young athletes are not the same and gives them specific guidance and tools to achieve success. As a high school and college basketball coach for over 30 years, I have found that many coaches and players continually get caught in the one size fits all concept. Jeff's straightforward examples and advice are outstanding and tend to get overlooked in today's youth sport society."

–Michael Mastroianni,
Athletic Director &
Head Boys Basketball Coach,
QUAKER VALLEY HIGH SCHOOL

The
Young Athlete's Guide to Playing Sports

The Young Athlete's Guide to Playing Sports

What Every Athlete Needs to Know to Play, Win, and Have Fun

JEFFREY RHOADS

AVAPLAY PRESS

AVAPLAY PRESS

Printed in Pittsburgh, Pennsylvania USA
First Edition: August 2013

ISBN: 978-0-9842113-2-6

Library of Congress Control Number: 2013908207

To the kids of Boncrest

Contents

PART III: YOUR PATH IN SPORTS

Preface
(for Parents)

When you were young, did you play sports? Whether you played competitively or simply for fun, I expect you answered yes. It's likely your parents would answer the same.

Young or old, player or fan, sports connect us with each other. They provide us with a powerful shared experience—one that crosses generations and appeals to people of wildly different backgrounds and circumstance.

This book is about how to play and enjoy sports. It's about teaching your child the essential elements of successful play. But it also provides you, the parent, with an opportunity to better understand and share this experience with your child. It can help you bridge differences and build a stronger parent/child bond—one not only based on love but also on working together to reach a common goal.

The Young Athlete's Guide to Playing Sports includes knowledge important to both beginners and young athletes who are more advanced. It covers fundamental principles that apply to all team sports, and many individual ones. It will help you convey to your child not only playing tips and techniques, but also positive values that will provide a lifetime of benefits. *The Young Athlete's Guide to Playing Sports* is both a compass to help you navigate you and your child's journey together in sports and a Swiss Army knife of essential knowledge; it can help you become a better pathfinder for your child's life in sports.

I've chosen a writing approach where each topic's instruction is addressed directly to the young athlete. (The "you" is your child.) My reason for doing so is twofold: First, you can more easily paraphrase a topic's information and incorporate it into the language you use to instruct your child. Secondly, for older children (age 13 and up) who enjoy reading and have an active interest in playing sports, you can give the book to them to read.

The book's chapters are organized into three parts: "Getting Started in Sports," "Becoming a Better Player," and "Your Path in Sports."

The first part, "Getting Started in Sports," contains topics relevant to the novice player. If your child is just starting out, you'll find valuable advice in this section regarding the fundamentals of successful play. You will also discover how your child can best learn sports skills. This part of the book also takes an in-depth look at pickup games. This form of sports play is unfortunately less prevalent now than in the past. But if you want your child to improve his or her play, fit in, and find more joy in playing sports, you need to understand these games and the benefits they provide.

The second part, "Becoming a Better Player," covers topics and approaches that will help young athletes improve their game. Intended for players of all skill levels, this section covers essential principles of play—the behaviors, strategies and tactics that support quality play. You will also discover how your son or daughter can better compete and what your child's coach wants to see in their play. This information can help bring your child greater competitive success and more playing time in games.

The third and final part, "Your Path in Sports," takes a more philosophical look at your child's journey through a life in sports. It's written for anyone who wants to better understand the forces that drive participation in sports. This part covers the role of parents, how they influence their child's sports experiences, and some of the problems a young athlete may encounter regarding their parents' attitudes and behavior. A discussion of why we play sports and how anyone can enjoy sports throughout their life is also included.

Some of the material I've included here originally appeared in my first book, *The Joy of Youth Sports*—a short book I wrote for parents. Describing "five steps to success," this other book provides parents with a concise overview of how to create the best youth sports experience for their child. You may find *The Joy of Youth Sports* a useful, quick read that complements the more detailed information contained in this book.

I have come to these writings through a lifetime of playing, coaching and enjoying sports. I've played competitive sports at both the high school and college level, played organized youth sports, enjoyed countless hours of pickup games, and coached youth basketball for more than twenty-five years. I've found joy in the simple act of playing, satisfaction in the pursuit of competitive success, and personal fulfillment in helping others learn how to play (and appreciate) sports. It's this wide breadth of experience that is the foundation of the advice I present in these pages—and possibly what sets this book apart from others that are more tightly focused on a single sport or perspective.

Many of the examples provided in this book come from my personal experience playing and coaching basketball; nevertheless, the principles they support are ones common to most team sports. Examples from other sports are also provided. I've also included several personal anecdotes that help illustrate the principles discussed. Your child may find inspiration in these stories.

Improving a child's opportunity in sports to have fun, develop skills, enjoy the shared experience, and possibly succeed in competitive sports, is a gift bestowed. I hope this book helps you bring this gift to *your* child.

Introduction

*"Winning is only half of it. Having
fun winning is the other half."*

*… Bum Phillips
(Football Coach)*

Almost everyone starts playing sports for a simple reason. It's fun. But have you ever thought about *why* playing a sport is fun?

Think for a moment about a few of the other activities in your life, ones that you enjoy and do well. Some may be simple, like riding your bike. Others may be more complex, like programming a computer, drawing a picture, or playing a musical instrument.

What attracts you to these activities? Although there are likely several reasons, they're fun partly because you *know* something about how to get a positive result. You've tasted some success.

Playing sports is no different. Knowing how to play a sport reasonably well, and achieving some success, makes playing more fun. And with fun and success, you're willing to work even harder to learn more and become better. The process reinforces itself. You learn more, play better, achieve more success, and have more fun.

Gaining knowledge is of course what this book is about. It aims to help you better understand the essential behaviors and principles of play that lead to success in *any* sport. Whether you're just starting out or you're a more advanced player looking to make your mark in competitive sports, this book can help you improve your game.

A few points about the organization of this book: Each chapter contains a series of stand-alone topics, all of which are listed by page number in the table of contents. You can jump to whatever topic interests you without necessarily reading the book cover to cover. A glossary of sports-related terms used within this book is included. If you are unfamiliar with a word or expression, flip to the back of the book.

To get the most out of this book, put the principles, practices, and examples included here to use. Don't just think about it—*do it*! Try stuff out as you practice and play games with your friends. Discover what works for you, and what doesn't. Grow your game. Have fun!

PART I:

Getting Started in Sports

Let's Play Ball!

Some of my friends seem more athletic than me. Do you have any tips on how I can move and react more quickly?

... Kyle

Everything has a beginning. If you're new to sports, or struggling to learn how to play a sport, you may be searching for that first foothold—the one from which you can gain traction and begin your upward climb toward excellence. You may be asking yourself, "Where do I start?"

So let's begin with the basics—some of the most important behaviors, principles, and guidelines that *every* player in *every* sport should know. With this information, you can get started the right way. You can set yourself up for success.

Fundamentals of Movement

The indispensable, ever-present element in sports is physical movement. To perform well, every athlete, in every sport, must efficiently execute body movements. Some of these relate to specific sports skills (fielding a groundball in baseball, hitting a tennis ball),

1

while others are more fundamental movements (running, jumping, changing direction) that are part of every sport's play.

Moving your *entire* body is done by managing your balance and applying force. Through countless hours of practice and play, you learn how to control both. You learn how to move efficiently, and do so without much conscious thought. As with other physical skills, movement benefits not only from practice, but also from personal attributes such as muscular strength, endurance, and your body type.

But proficient body movement begins with a simple principle. And what's especially attractive to the average athlete, is that you don't need physical gifts or hours of practice to put this principle to good use. Instead you simply need to focus your attention on applying it.

The ready position

This primary principle is: *Body movement is most efficiently initiated from a position of readiness that enables quick movement in any direction.*

You see it in every sport. From defensive stances to the starting positions in which a ball is struck, all good athletes initiate movement from a general body pose. Known as the *ready position,* it's an athletic position typified by the following characteristics:

- Feet spread, shoulder width apart (or wider)

- Knees slightly bent

- Back bent slightly forward at the waist with the shoulders retracted back and down, and head up

- Arms hanging down to the side of the body with elbows flexed, hands at hip level, and the palms facing inward

How does this athletic "ready" position help you move more efficiently? It provides you with the balance needed to begin moving (or resist being moved). Spreading your feet establishes a base of support; bending your knees lowers your center of gravity to strengthen that base; bending your back slightly forward helps keep your weight centered over the balls of your feet; the position of your arms helps you fine tune balance adjustments (and prepares you to more quickly catch a ball, defend a pass, etc.).

With control of your balance, you have better control of the forces needed to initiate movement. You can quickly execute a forceful push-off against a stable base. Balance control also enables you to use *instability* to begin moving. By purposely losing your balance, you use the pull of gravity to begin moving. (Think of a track sprinter who falls forward out of the blocks.)

This position also loads the spring (partially stretches your muscles) for explosive release. With knees slightly bent, you're ready to move. You don't have to first bend legs that are straight. And this means that the time required to initiate a movement (the preparatory phase) is shortened; you begin running or jumping more quickly. Where a more forceful movement is needed, you've already begun loading your muscles; by further bending your knees you add more force.

So if you have a tendency to stand around during play, waiting to receive a pass with legs straight, hands at your side—assume the ready position! Bend your knees, shift your weight forward

● ☆Beginners who are unsure of themselves have a tendency to stick their hands in their pockets. Not only does this behavior show a lack of confidence, but it also detracts from a player's performance. Keep your hands out of your pockets and ready for action!

▶ An extension of the ready position used in tennis and other sports is the *split-step*. This technique uses a small two-footed hop to load the ready position and enable a quicker, more explosive initial reaction. Watch a professional tennis match to see how each player uses it before almost every return. Baseball fielders, soccer goalies, and volleyball players also use this hop step technique to get a "jump" on the ball.

slightly, and get your arms and hands up and ready. And then watch how much quicker you can receive that pass and begin moving your body.

Varying your start-up position

Although the basic ready position provides the balance and muscle stretch needed to efficiently initiate many movements, an athlete's *actual* starting position varies depending on the sport and situation.

Some variations obviously relate to the sports skill itself. For instance, a baseball hitter and golfer's hands are not at their side; they need to respectively grip a bat and golf club. A basketball player, playing in a zone defense, will likely have his arms extended upward and outward to more easily deny passing lanes. (But in all of these instances the lower body is still in the athletic position.)

Most other variations stem from an athlete's need to react more quickly in certain directions to a specific threat. Here are some examples:

- A tennis player returning a serve, needing to move quickly from side to side, usually assumes a very wide stance.

- A defensive back in football, more concerned with a receiver running past him, will usually place one foot ahead of the other instead of side to side (like a football linebacker).

- A basketball player defending a quick opponent who drives to the hoop, might also place one foot ahead of the other, along with shifting his or her weight slightly more backward. Since basketball play depends heavily on the use of an athlete's hands and arms, a basketball player would also initially extend his or her arms slightly more outward.

In all of these situations, the athletes change their ready position as needed to best counter an opponent's advantage. They evaluate the situation and apply the appropriate technique. To move quickly in *any* direction, they assume a more neutral startup position (the basic ready position). And to react even *more* quickly to a specific threat, they change their startup position to emphasize movement in one or two directions.

Finally, notice that you control your start-up position *before* the action begins. You usually have plenty of time to set yourself up. You just need to know how to modify your athletic position based on the situation.

Body position during movement

When you run, jump, or change direction, you do so by constantly shifting your balance. Learning how to do this well typically requires much practice and play. But similar to the ready position, there's a simple principle that you can easily apply. Bend your knees!

By bending your knees while moving, you lower your center of gravity (COG) and improve your balance. This not only helps you react more quickly to the unexpected, but also helps you pivot and change direction.[1]

Try it yourself. Run in a small rectangular path (for example around the rectangular part of the "Key" on a basketball court), making perpendicular cuts at each corner. First try running in a normal motion with legs relatively straight. Next, exaggerate your knee bend each time you change direction. Lower your hips and body just as you're planting your outside foot. Then pivot on the balls of your feet so that you're facing the new direction. Notice how your balance control increases as you lower your COG. Your base of support is more stable and it's easier to get a good push-off as you pivot and begin to accelerate into a more upright position.

If you believe that your movements are slower compared to your friends, focus more on bending your knees when you change directions and pivot. (You may find it easier to think of dropping your hips.) By learning to raise and lower your COG as needed, your movement will become more effective.

How an athletic position helps you avoid injury

Not only does bending your knees put your body in the proper athletic position to move, it also helps prevent injury. Some of the more serious knee injuries in sports are the result of the extreme forces associated with an athlete planting a leg to stop, land (from a jump), or change direction. In these cases, your knees are less susceptible to injury when your legs are bent. This is because bending your knees activates the surrounding muscles which, in turn, help absorb force. With legs straight, this protection is absent; all of the force is absorbed by your knee's ligaments and tendons.

Since you can also react more quickly from an athletic position, you can more easily avoid potential collisions. While moving, you can more rapidly change direction. From the stationary ready position, you can more quickly begin to move. And with hands ready, you can also better defend your upper body—most importantly your head. For example, volleyball players with arms down and hands by their side cannot react fast enough to protect against an opponent's hard spike. But with hands ready, you can avoid a painful and embarrassing hit to your head, and possibly make a play on the ball.

Keep Your Head Up

When dribbling a ball, it's not unusual for a beginning soccer or basketball player to constantly look down at it—especially when closely defended. Similarly, beginning hockey players often need to look at the puck as they push it up the ice. This behavior is understandable as these players have not yet developed the necessary ball and puck handling skills.

Unfortunately, more advanced players often demonstrate the same behavior. When under pressure or trying to score they turn their head downwards, exerting all their concentration and effort on advancing the ball or puck past their immediate defender(s).

The problem with this behavior is that success in sports often depends on knowing where teammates and opponents are located, where advantage and disadvantage situations exist, and how best to get the ball or puck to, and into, the goal.

To recognize opportunities and play your best, you must be able to *see* the entire playing field, court, or ice—and that means keeping your head up whenever possible. The ability to do so, especially when trying to control a ball or puck against defensive pressure, depends on your skill level and confidence. You must become comfortable performing these skills while focusing your attention around you and elsewhere.

How do you develop this ability? Even without watching a moving object, your mind has an amazing capacity to know where the object will be. Absent visual information, your mind turns to other senses. A *kinesthetic* sense of body position and *visuospatial* perception of spatial relationships take over. They create within your mind's eye an awareness of an object's location in time and space.

Although the ability to use these senses is challenging at first, you can develop it over time. You just need to repetitively practice your skills, *reducing visual input as you become more proficient.* Initially, try to use your peripheral vision instead of looking directly at the object you are controlling. Then extend the time you perform the skill with your head up and vision focused elsewhere. (For instance, while dribbling a ball, talk to someone and look directly at their face.)

Becoming more aware

But what if you don't yet have the ability to perform certain skills without looking at the ball? How can you still succeed when you have difficulty controlling the ball or puck against aggressive defenders?

Well, keeping your head up gives you other advantages. First, it enables you to recognize defensive pressure *before* it's applied. And by doing so, you can often *avoid* more difficult situations. By keeping your head up, knowing who is open, and passing the ball or puck to a teammate before your defenders arrive, you preempt the pressure. You avoid the potential turnover. And even lacking outstanding ball or puck handling skills, you still succeed.

Secondly, keeping your head up also can lead to better *scoring opportunities* for both you and your teammates. Passing to an open player closer to the goal is almost always the easiest way to score. But if your head is down, you waste these opportunities.

Closer to the goal, the same principle applies. As you drive toward the goal, you will likely draw defenders toward you. If your head is up and eyes forward, you can recognize opportunities to make a pass to an open teammate for an easy goal. And should you see the defender retreating to cover your teammate, you can instead attempt to score the goal yourself.

▶ Although you want to keep your head up in most sports, *golf* is not one of them!

Also, by keeping your head up you see all of the little clues that can provide you or your team with an opportunity to gain advantage. For example, you may see that a teammate's defender is overplaying the passing lane and is susceptible to a backdoor cut. At the same time, your teammate may move his eyes or make some other subtle gesture to let you know that he also recognizes the same opportunity and wants you to be ready to make the pass.

Finally, you *must* keep your head up to avoid injury. In contact sports such as hockey or football, collisions between players (intentional and unintentional) are part of the game. To lessen their impact and to avoid hurtful hits, you must be aware of player movements and recognize potentially dangerous situations *before* they occur. Likewise, you also need to be aware of balls, pucks, or other fast moving objects that can cause injury.

So if you want to play your best, and not be sidelined by injury, keep your head up!

Use Your Peripheral Vision

To track both the action *around* the ball and player movements *away* from the ball, you sometimes need to quickly turn your head back and forth. This is especially true when the ball and players of interest are not all in front of you.

But when all of the action is within your field of view, a more effective technique is to use your *peripheral vision*. This is the part of vision that occurs outside the very center of your gaze, and extends to the edges of your field of view.

When using your peripheral vision, you never lose sight of a potentially key event (unlike turning your head back and forth). You can track all of the action all of the time. By seeing both the action around the ball and your opponent, you can anticipate and react quicker to play better defense. Similarly, on offense, you can recognize passing and scoring opportunities without having to look directly at your teammates. You can see a teammate off to your side cutting toward the goal, even as you attack your defender.

How do you use your peripheral vision? Instead of focusing your line of sight directly on one player (or the ball), look in a direction that is half-way between two players. Although you will not see either player clearly, you can still recognize their movements. And this is the key information you need to react. Depending on the relative importance of each player (and how close they are to the edges of your field of view), you can also shift your line of sight slightly one way or the other.

To become more aware of your peripheral vision, try this simple exercise. Extend both of your arms fully outward to your sides at eye level and wiggle your fingers. *While focusing on an object in front of you*, slowly move your arms forward until you begin to see your fingers. Notice that you only see the *movement* of your fingers—

everything else has no clear shape! You can move your hands forward and backward to explore the edges of your field of view and increase your awareness of this type of vision.

Using your peripheral vision (on defense)

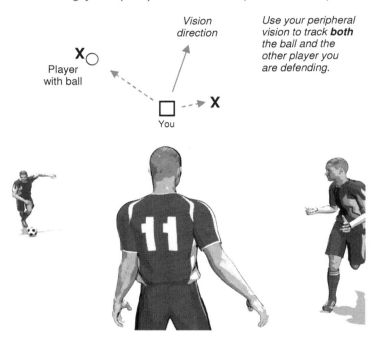

Although the above diagram illustrates how the defender uses his peripheral vision, consider how the same approach is used by the attacking player with the ball. As he moves forward, he is primarily looking at the defender while also using his peripheral vision to track both the ball and the position of his teammate on the opposite side.

Finally, using your peripheral vision not only helps improve your play, but also prevents injury. Keeping your head up, "on a swivel" (moving your head back and forth), and actively using your peripheral vision, all help you anticipate events *before* they happen. By recognizing approaching players and objects early, you can react more quickly to avoid dangerous collisions.

Focus on the Target

You probably know that you need to focus on a target when you pass, shoot, or hit a ball. When you first learned to catch a ball, you undoubtedly were instructed to "keep your eyes on the ball." By focusing your eyes on a target, you engage your mind's visuospatial ability. (*Visuospatial* is the perception of the spatial relationships among objects within the field of vision.) You know when and where the ball, person, or other object will be. And in turn, this triggers the appropriate physical response. With practice, you swing a bat at the right time in the right place. You put your hands or glove where the ball will arrive. If you're shooting, you apply the precise amount of force in the right direction to get the ball to and in the goal.

So how does this "targeting" process work and how can you improve it?

You may believe that all you need to do is focus on the ball, goal, or player. But here's an important question that you need to ask yourself, "*What* target am I aiming for?" It's not quite as simple as you may think.

If you're shooting a basketball, the general target is the basketball rim. If it's the *entire* basketball hoop, however, your mind's subconscious targeting mechanism is focused on the ball hitting the hoop. That, of course, is not your real "goal." You want the ball to go *through* the hoop!

Like a paper shooting target, you need to find and focus on a bulls-eye. Why? Because your accuracy improves when you *narrow* your focus. You provide your mind with a more exact target. And this, in turn, fine-tunes the mind's targeting mechanism.

You want the target to be as small as possible. Besides triggering a more efficient and accurate targeting response, it also has a side-benefit. There's more room for error. If you "miss," you can still achieve your primary objective—scoring a goal or making a pass that your teammate can handle.

Here are some examples of targets you can use in different sports. Instead of aiming for that basketball hoop, use one of the hoop's metal hooks as your physical reference point. Your mind will lock in on the smaller target, and your results will improve.

For larger goals, such as those in hockey or soccer, you can use the edges of the goal as your baseline target. You can then create a mental map of smaller imaginary targets slightly inside these edges. In practice, you can use corner targets, shooting tarps, or place plastic cones in the spots you want to hit.

For passes, also select an appropriate small target. It may be the emblem at the center of your teammate's shirt or your teammate's hands. In baseball, it's likely your teammate's glove. In hockey, it's often the blade of a stick. Sometimes the spot you aim for is one located on the court, field, or ice. You may need to pass to where a teammate will be, not where they are now. In a sport like tennis, you want to aim for specific spots on the court. When serving, for example, don't simply aim for the service box. Instead, narrow your focus and aim for a corner of the box.

▶ When *receiving* a pass, provide your teammate with a target. Extend your hands or glove. Put your hockey stick blade on the ice.

Communicate in Team Sports

If you're new to a sport, you may be shy and fearful of making mistakes. To avoid being the center of attention, you may say little, speak in a low voice, or unintelligibly mutter your words.

This type of behavior presents a problem in team sports. Team play *always* benefits from players who communicate with each other. You need to realize the importance of talking to your teammates as game situations unfold.

For example, when playing man-to-man defense in basketball, communication between the players is essential. Players must call out screens. The player defending the ball must sometimes call out defensive switches or ask for help.

Many coaches view the failure of players to communicate as an unacceptable mental mistake. There's no room for shyness when it comes to players communicating with their teammates during a game. Speak up!

▶ When you communicate, you need to SHOUT words loudly with emotional emphasis ("PICK LEFT!"). You need to do this both in games and practice. Even if you're not directly involved in the action, you can still let your teammate know that something is about to happen.

Play with the Right Attitude

Physical ability, sports skills, and a command of game tactics all help determine how successful you are playing a sport. But unless you also approach your practice and play with the right *attitude*, it's unlikely you will achieve success over the long run.

Your attitude affects every aspect of your game including how you prepare, how you play, and how well you compete in more difficult contests. It also affects your relationships with teammates and coaches.

If you enjoy your sport, practice becomes more fun. And even when it's not a lot of fun, keeping in mind the goal you are pursuing helps make your hard work and sacrifice more meaningful. A positive attitude helps your play. You execute sports skills better when you're confident and relaxed, playing within the flow of the game and focusing on each moment. A positive attitude also helps you overcome challenging odds, possibly beating a better opponent or staging an incredible comeback. With a good attitude, your teammates will respect you and turn to you for leadership. And especially important in competitive organized sports, your coaches will want you on their team.

What are some characteristics of players who have a good attitude? Here are a few of the more important ones:

- Believe in themselves, not just in their ability to play but also in their ability to learn and improve.

- Willing to listen, learn, accept team roles, and make the necessary sacrifices to become better.

- Never gives up, regardless of the score.

- Relishes difficult challenges as an opportunity to play their best.

- Supports their teammates, always looking to make them better players.

- Acknowledges mistakes, but doesn't blame others or dwell too long on what's done. Translates negative events immediately into a positive response.

- Respects everyone and everything associated with the game including opponents, coaches, officials, and the rules.

Now for the bad

So what about the players who have a *poor* attitude?

Often their negative attitude results from a lack of skills and inability to compete. These players are trying (or tried), but are unable to connect their effort to any real success. They become frustrated and eventually start expecting to fail.

For many of these young players, however, a less than positive attitude may only be temporary. As their bodies mature and their skills develop, they begin to experience more success. And consequently, their attitude toward playing improves.

Unfortunately, there are more serious defects of attitude, ones that can permanently undermine an athlete's opportunity to succeed. Here are a few to avoid:

- Refuses to be accountable for mistakes; plays the "victim" role, always blaming others when they fail.

- Constantly criticizes teammates, sometimes undermining them to gain advantage.

- Is arrogant and disrespectful toward others, including the team's coach.

- Refuses to listen and learn from others.

- Selfishly pursues individual goals at the expense of the team.

- Expects to lose.

💣 Other players don't enjoy playing with individuals who exhibit these negative qualities. Coaches usually do not want these types of players on their team.

Finally, remember that your attitude toward playing sports is largely under your control. Everyone messes up from time to time—makes a mistake and acts out. But try to recognize some of your weaknesses in this area, develop a healthier outlook, and behave in ways that reflect and build upon your positive attitude.

Trust Your Skills (Don't Think Too Much)

As you progress in your sport, you will receive instruction from many sources including your parents, coaches, other players, videos, and books. To learn a new skill (or correct one that is deficient), you need to understand the fundamental movements that comprise the skill and how these movements flow together in a coordinated sequence. You will need to initially think about the skill, break it down, and analyze your execution of it.

When you're competing, however, it's essential that you *trust the skills that you have learned and practiced.* As the Nike motto says, you need to "Just Do It!"

You cannot think about how you will execute a skill during a game. If you do, you obstruct the subconscious body-mind connection that you've developed through hours of practice. This will slow reaction time and often destroy the natural flow needed to properly execute a skill. Likewise, observing yourself (as if you were a third person watching you) will also hurt your ability to perform well.

Confidence and positive imagery is instead the key to success. You must know that the ball will go in, and see it doing so in your mind's eye. See yourself executing each skill with perfect form—without thinking through every step. Live in the moment of these images. *Picture your success.*

For example, broad or triple jumpers in track need to get their approach steps down properly to achieve the longest jump. The last step should ideally land immediately before the far edge of the takeoff board. By repeating successful approaches and takeoffs in practice, the mechanics of

▶ To let "muscle memory" take over, incorporate trigger movements at the beginning of the skill. In golf, "waggle" the club's head before beginning your backswing. For a basketball free throw, you might bounce the basketball four times to engage your body and then exhale immediately before beginning the actual shooting motion.

this skill are ingrained within a jumper. Thinking about *how* this is done during a track meet will only inhibit the body's ability to do what it has been trained to do. Instead, a jumper needs to cast away any doubts about footwork and envision a perfect approach, takeoff, jump, and final result.

When I played basketball in high school and college, I always approached the free throw line thinking that these "gimme" points were mine and envisioned the ball going through the hoop. Once I had begun the initial movement of my shooting motion, I would clear my mind, focus on the target, and let the hours of practice take over.

Practice your skills to the point that you don't need to think about how you perform them. Trust your skills and play your game with confidence knowing that your body will follow your mind's eye to the result you see and desire.

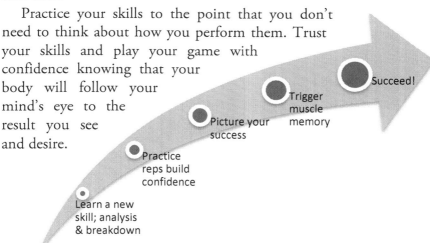

Succeed!

Trigger muscle memory

Picture your success

Practice reps build confidence

Learn a new skill; analysis & breakdown

Conditioning

To play sports well, you can't depend on talent and skills alone. Knowledge, athleticism, highly developed sports skills, are all important attributes that support your play. But sports *are* physical. Unless your body is conditioned, your ability will eventually crumble under the weight of fatigue. As you learn how to play sports, you also need to learn how to keep your body in good physical condition.

Although an in-depth discussion of conditioning techniques is beyond the scope of this book, here are a few general principles to keep in mind:

- *Each sport requires both a broad level of fitness **and** physical conditioning that is specific to the sport itself.* Although you may be in shape in one sport, this conditioning doesn't necessarily translate to another. In your preseason training, you need to focus your physical preparation on the types of movements specific to your sport. Besides playing, use training routines that develop the strength and endurance your sport requires. If you play multiple sports, consider selecting ones that physically complement each other.

  I learned this lesson when I ran cross-country my senior year in high school, believing that it would help get me in shape for basketball. Instead, I struggled during the initial three days of basketball tryouts. Although my body was in shape for distance running, it was ill-prepared for the short, explosive sprints that are ever-present in basketball. A sport such as soccer would have better conditioned my body for playing basketball.

- *Your performance will improve most when you train yourself in three key areas: (1) cardiovascular (running, swimming, cycling), (2) strength (calisthenics, weight-lifting), and (3) flexibility (stretching).* Although you may concentrate more on one area to correct a deficiency, you want to balance all three elements. Not only will this benefit your overall performance, it will also help prevent injuries. (e.g., strength can help protect your joints, stretching can reduce muscle pulls). Besides these three key areas, speed, agility and balance drills will also help improve your performance in many sports.

- *Cross-training is a beneficial training technique that involves training your body using different activities (ones that engage different muscle groups).* For example, you might complement playing soccer with secondary activities of swimming and biking. By alternating your training activities you can both improve your general fitness and protect against overuse injuries (those that occur from performing the same stressful physical movement many times). Also, playing one sport can sometimes help improve a specific skill in another sport. For instance, playing tennis can help improve your footwork. This can translate to quicker movements on the soccer field or basketball court. Playing volleyball will improve your vertical jump—an ability that will likely help you rebound better in basketball.

- *For quickly developing cardiovascular conditioning suitable to many team sports, use* **interval training**. This technique involves bursts of high intensity effort intermixed with short periods of recovery. For example, you can sprint around three sides of a soccer field and walk one of the end lines.

- *Strength is more than simply how much of something you can lift. It also involves endurance (how many times you can lift an object) and explosive power (the force and velocity with which you move yourself or an object).* Your training programs should focus on all three aspects. Lifting more weight with fewer repetitions will improve your maximum capacity and muscle size. Lifting lesser weight, but with more repetitions, will help improve your endurance. Performing exercises that require maximal force in minimal time, such as box jumps to improve jumping, will generate more explosive strength.

  Also keep in mind that different forms of strength training (barbells, dumbbells, machines, calisthenics) all train your body differently. For example, doing bench presses using dumbbells will typically engage more supporting muscle groups than the same exercise performed on a Nautilus machine. This characteristic sometimes more closely duplicates the type of strength needed to play sports.

- *Core stability is essential to better sports performance.* Because sports skills are often performed off balance, greater core stability provides a foundation for increased force production in an athlete's upper and lower extremities. To improve your core stability, you need to strengthen your abdominal and other trunk muscles, and ideally in a way that transfers to your sport. Since many sports skills are performed from a standing body position, ground-based resistance exercises (e.g., lifting dumbbells) may best improve your sports-specific core stability. This approach is also more time efficient; you're simultaneously strengthening your core, arms, and legs. [2]

- *Begin and end each workout with warm-up and warm-down periods.* In your warm-up, perform some activity (shoot baskets, jog, lift light weights) that prepares your body for the heavy exertion to follow. Break a sweat. Once you're warmed up, spend a few minutes stretching your body in ways specific to your upcoming activity. For instance, if your sport involves sprinting, lightly stretch your hamstring muscles. Warming-down is simply the reverse of warming-up. When your workout is ending, you can slowly reduce your level of exertion. For example, when you've finished running hard, slow to a jog, and then continue walking. When you're done, take some time to stretch your muscles. This is the safest and most beneficial time to stretch (and improve your flexibility).

Numerous books and videos are available that describe exercises, drills, and programs to help get you in shape. Many of these also provide advice on how to train for specific sports. Besides learning training techniques from your friends and coaches, take advantage of these resources.

Taking Care of Your Body

Besides getting in shape to play sports, you also need to take care of your body in other ways. You need to pay attention to what you eat and drink, get the necessary rest, and deal with any injuries that occur.

Nutrition for athletes

For you to play your best, you must provide your body with the necessary fuel. For most young athletes, a balanced diet coupled with the proper hydration is all that's needed. But there are a few ways to maximize your performance as it relates to your nutrition. Here are some key points that you should consider:

- *When you eat a pregame meal can affect your performance.* Two to four hours before a competition is a rough guideline with larger meals eaten earlier. Your goal is to have enough energy to comfortably last through your contest. However, you want to avoid an upset stomach or sluggishness that can result from eating too much too close to the start of your competition. Experiment to determine what works best for you.

- *What you eat in your pregame meal can affect your performance.* You should eat a smaller meal heavy in starch carbohydrates and light in fats and protein. This will maximize the energy available to you throughout your contest. An example of a good pregame meal is pasta, bread, and a salad with low-fat dressing. Many sports nutritionists recommend a calorie balance of approximately 60% Carbohydrates, 20% Protein, and 20% Fat (60/20/20). Avoid high-sugar foods (candy, donuts) that can trigger a surge of insulin that leads to a sharp drop in blood sugar. Again, experiment to discover *your* optimum pregame meal.

- *Dehydration can worsen your performance.* Proper fluid replenishment is essential! Dehydration reduces the volume of blood circulating, causing muscles to receive less oxygen and performance to suffer. Water is sufficient for most sports activities of average duration. Drink fluids before, during, and after a workout or contest. Also, be aware that thirst is not always a good indicator of dehydration. Urine that is dark gold in color is a sign of dehydration.

- *Fluid replacement drinks (e.g., Gatorade, etc.) may improve performance in certain situations.* These drinks help hydrate your body, provide glucose (sugar), sodium (salt), and potassium. Although your body does not require additional glucose for the first 45-90 minutes, intense exercise exceeding this time may require that you consume additional carbohydrates. Studies suggest that drinks having a carbohydrate concentration between 6-8 percent are the most effective.

- *Consuming carbohydrates and protein shortly after a workout may promote muscle repair and improve your recovery time.* Some studies have shown that consuming carbohydrates within 30 minutes after exercise can improve recovery time. (An additional carbohydrate meal should also follow within 2 hours.) Some research also suggests that 10-20 grams of high quality protein shortly after exercise may be beneficial.

- *Supplements are unlikely to improve your performance.* Although you will likely hear your friends talk about the benefits of protein, vitamin, and other supplements, studies have consistently shown that they are no more effective than a balanced diet. Also, the supplement industry is loosely regulated, and the quality of the products is not guaranteed. If you are extremely active and have difficulty consuming the necessary amount of food to maintain your weight, a protein/carbohydrate supplement may help.

Besides the above points, a wealth of more detailed information is available online. If you're interested in improving your nutrition and learning more about how it affects athletic performance, start by going to government websites such as the President's Council on Fitness, Sports & Nutrition (www.fitness.gov), and the USDA websites (www.nutrition.gov, www.choosemyplate.gov). An online search (e.g., "nutrition athlete") will produce many links that you can explore.

Getting your rest

Your ability to train, increase your strength and endurance, and consistently perform your best in competitions, requires that you provide your body with the necessary rest. "Rest" encompasses both the recovery time you provide between workouts and the amount of sleep you get each night.

When you train your body (running, weightlifting, etc.), you break down muscle fiber. With adequate recovery time, your muscles restore themselves. Resistance training uses this principle to build strength. With the right combination of exercise and rest, your muscles rebuild themselves even stronger than before. But if you don't get enough rest, you short-circuit this process. In the typical weight-lifting program, you should provide 48 hours of rest between training sessions. By training different muscle groups on different days, you can obtain the necessary rest, but still work out.

Recovery time is important in virtually every sport. Athletes "peak" for important events, training themselves harder early on and reducing their workout load shortly before an event takes place. For any important game, match, or meet, don't over-train the day before. Give your body a chance to recover and store up its resources.

It should be obvious to you *the importance of sleep.* Anyone who's stayed up most of the night at a sleepover or cramming for a test knows how they felt the next day. Reaction times slow, perception is altered, and concentration is often more difficult. Moreover, studies suggest that sleep deprivation impairs your body. Muscles, broken down from the prior day's training, are not fully restored. Cardiovascular performance is reduced and the ability of the body to break down and use glucose is slowed. Hormonal levels are affected in a way that can lead to increased appetite and weight gain.

If you want to perform your best, you must try to regularly get an adequate amount of sleep (8-10 hours per night). Make it a priority—keep a regular sleep schedule. Your room should be dark, cool, and free of noise. Avoid late-night distractions like smartphones, computers, and TV. Also, avoid caffeinated energy drinks in the evening.

Dealing with injuries

Playing sports inevitably brings with it some injuries. Most are minor—the occasional bumps and bruises that accompany any physical activity.

But the more you play, the more likely it is that you will suffer an injury that will temporarily take you away from your sport. Sprained ankles and pulled muscles are the usual culprits. For these types of injuries, R.I.C.E. (rest, icing, compression, and elevation) is the regimen you should follow to more quickly return to your sport. Here's what experts recommend:

- To reduce swelling, apply ice as soon as possible to the injury and continue intermittently over the next 24 hours. Apply for 15-20 minutes each hour. To protect your skin, place a thin towel between the ice and injury. (Freezable cold wraps are especially convenient; keep a few in your refrigerator's freezer compartment.)

- Compression also helps reduce the swelling that can impede healing. Firmly wrap the injury with an elastic bandage. Be careful not to cut off the blood supply by wrapping too tightly.

- Elevate the injured arm or leg above the level of your heart.

- Give your body a chance to heal! Depending on the severity of your injury, reduce any load or impact that can aggravate the injury. Once the initial swelling has subsided, do range-of-motion stretching exercises to regain flexibility. (For instance, draw letters of the alphabet in space with your injured foot, hand, or finger.) Some experts believe that early mobilization helps ligaments and tendons heal faster; for these types of injuries, you may want to immediately begin some limited, protected movement. As the healing process continues, begin strengthening exercises to regain your former strength. Moist heat and massage may also help the healing process at this point. When you return to your sport, protect the injured body part. For a sprain, you may want to initially wear an elastic wrap or brace. Start slow and gradually build back up to your normal level of activity.

For the typical sprain or other soft tissue injury, you will normally see a reduction in swelling over the first 24 hours. If after 48 hours you don't see an improvement, it's time to contact a doctor.

Occasionally, more serious injuries occur. These can include head trauma (concussion), broken bones, or torn ligaments in a joint. These of course are ones that take longer to heal and require a doctor's attention.

Should you get injured more seriously, it's usually only a matter of time before you're back on the field. With today's medical technology, almost every serious injury is fixable. The most difficult aspect of these injuries is often the recovery period—being away from your sport and patiently waiting for your body to heal.

Get Your Gear

Playing sports is exciting. Most of that feeling comes from playing the games themselves. But it's also fun when you get a new baseball glove, basketball, skates, or pair of athletic shoes. Seeing yourself in your team uniform at the beginning of each season is exciting. (Yes, you look good!)

But beyond the thrill of getting some new sports gear, you need to pay attention to what really matters when it comes to selecting your gear: *Do you have equipment that both protects you and helps you perform to the best of your ability?*

Safety first

Especially in contact sports such as football or hockey, quality equipment is important for your safety. Helmets, mouth guards, and padding all help protect you against injury. Wearing quality gear that is sized correctly is essential.

You need to respect this aspect of playing sports. Don't forget to wear your mouth guard, buckle straps, and tie your shoes. Use protective equipment as it was designed. As mentioned in the prior topic, injury can keep you away from your sport for an extended period. And that's not fun!

Gear up for performance

Does equipment affect your performance? Sometimes it does; other times not so much.

Obviously, you're putting yourself at a disadvantage if you wear worn out shoes that can't grip the playing surface. Likewise, cheap equipment that quickly breaks down isn't going to help your performance. You don't want any of your gear to fail during a game.

Sometimes using *ill-fitted equipment* can hurt your ability to perform well. A tennis racquet's grip may be too large for your small hands, making it harder for you to change grips and get wrist snap on your serve. Too small of a grip and the racquet will twist in your hand and require more strength to control. A baseball bat may be too heavy for you to control and swing quickly. Too light of a bat and you will sacrifice power. In each of these cases, the gear is a poor fit for your physical makeup.

You can also choose the wrong type of gear for your *position or style of play*. When I played quarterback as a freshman in high school I wore the bulky shoulder pads that almost everybody on the team wore. But the father of one boy bought him some special quarterback shoulder pads. Although there were other more significant reasons why my career as a high school quarterback was short-lived, those pads probably gave him a little extra advantage throwing the football.

Does expensive equipment *always* help improve your play? No. Athletic skill usually trumps equipment design—as long as the gear is reasonably good. An excellent tennis player who plays with a mediocre racquet will still beat a lesser opponent playing with the best racquet available.

With regard to cost, here are a couple of other points to keep in mind. Although properly fitted quality equipment does ensure that your performance isn't hurt by the gear itself, you can often find excellent gear at a lower cost. Sometimes you're paying for a brand's name, reputation, and advertising costs. A lesser known manufacturer may produce quality equipment and sell it at a more reasonable price. Also, be aware that performance gains are typically much less at the top end. You will usually get much more performance value moving from a low cost piece of gear to one of average quality than you will by buying the best possible gear. And in some cases, only the best players will benefit from the features and qualities of the most expensive equipment.

▶ Be realistic about whether you're likely to change sports or lose interest. You don't need the best equipment to see if you enjoy playing a sport. You can always upgrade your equipment later. (But where safety is important, don't sacrifice quality.)

Function over form

Most players like to look good. Cool shoes and nice uniforms all make us feel a little better about ourselves as we hit the field or court. But keep in mind, playing sports is still about the play itself. Don't get too caught up in your equipment and how you look. Get the gear that fits and matches your ability. Wear the right protective equipment. And most importantly, focus on your play!

Sportsmanship, Respect, and Character

When we talk about *sportsmanship*, we're usually referring to the respect we show others. But respect has an even wider meaning. It encompasses how you treat everyone and everything that comprises your experience in sports.

Early on, you must learn to respect coaches, teammates, opponents, officials, the rules of the game, *and yourself.* Each of these helps form your personal experience in sports.

In team sports, success is most often based on the collective efforts of many players and a coach. Each participant plays a different role. Each should respect and acknowledge the other's contributions, and where possible, help enable others to more effectively play their part. The best players make their teammates better. Ask yourself on occasion whether you make your teammates better as both players and individuals.

● Cheating or "bending the rules" during a contest undermines this structure—sometimes to the point where the competition itself is ruined. This is especially true in neighborhood pickup games that depend on the interest of its participants to keep the game going. Respect your game's rules!

Your opponents are part of the same community, sharing similar values and goals. Each opponent provides the competition that can potentially bring out the best in you. Always respect your opponent. As the saying goes, "Be humble in victory and gracious in defeat."

The game and its rules must also be respected. Sports are essentially structured play, where participants agree to adhere to a set of rules that both define the game and promote fair competition.

And lastly, you need to respect yourself. To play your best, you must respect your body—taking care of it in the ways described in the previous topics. By establishing good practice habits, and competing to the best of your ability, you also build the self-respect and confidence that every successful athlete must possess.

How you play affects other's view of you

Everyone who plays sports likes to win. Winning is a tangible benchmark of your effort to realize your potential—to become the best you can be. Winning helps bring you both internal rewards (joy, satisfaction) and external ones (awards, peer recognition). Winning is a worthy goal.

But how you pursue this goal—the way in which you play the game—says a lot about the nature of your character; who you are, the principles you believe in, and what you will do to back up those beliefs. And over time, your behavior affects how others view you.

If you compete fairly, with skill and determination, you will gain the respect of your opponents. Practice and play to the best of your ability, and you will earn the admiration of your teammates and coaches. Lead others, making each of them better people in the process, and you will win their loyalty. Combine all of these qualities with a measure of humility and respect, and others will speak of your greatness.

Learning How to Play

*I'm just starting out in sports. How can I
learn new skills and improve my game?*

... Jenny

To play sports, you need to develop a set of basic skills. You need to understand fundamental principles of individual and team play. And to play sports *well*, you must also learn less-obvious rules of conduct—those non-athletic behaviors that are crucial to success.

How do you best acquire these skills and knowledge? This chapter will help answer that question. We'll start with a general overview of the learning process as it relates to playing sports. Then, we'll take a look at specific learning techniques (for instance, how to learn a skill by first breaking it down into parts and then using repetition to lock it in).

One last point before we begin. Knowing *how to learn* is not only a key to playing sports better, but also a valuable life skill. It's a lever that amplifies your ability to become proficient in *any* endeavor. It helps make you more self-reliant and extends your opportunity to realize your full potential. And when applied to sports, it provides you with the capacity to continuously improve your skill set and overall game—beyond the specific skills that any one source can teach you.

Learning the Basics

How did you first learn how to play a sport? If you're like most kids, your parents, coaches, and friends provided you with some basic instruction. They taught you both the rules and essential skills. As you progressed, these people continued to play an instrumental role in teaching you how to better play a sport. They helped you refine your individual sports skills and learn more advanced ones. In team sports, they taught you those skills (passing, screening, moving without the ball, communication) that enabled you to play better with teammates. Under the guidance of these early influences, you began to also acquire an understanding of strategy, tactics, and patterns of play—the actions and reactions that affect your opportunity to succeed against an opponent.

At some point, you also started to expand your understanding of sports beyond the explicit instruction of others. You began to play a greater direct role in your own education. Through personal observation you may have emulated other players to learn a new move or sports skill. By observing others, you also learned the culture of your sport; how a player's behavior either led to acceptance by one's teammates, or made that player the one nobody wanted to play with.

And as you gained more experience, you began to see how various non-athletic factors affect how well you play a sport. How attitude impacts performance. How preparation leads to success. You also started to learn your strengths and weaknesses—and if you were really aware, how to maximize the former and compensate for the latter. Much of this learning likely occurred naturally as a byproduct of your play.

But if you want to improve your play further, it may be time to go beyond simply being a passive participant, absorbing knowledge as it happens to come your way. You may now need to take a more proactive role in your education.

One of your first steps in doing so is to *choose how and where you practice and play*. Why? Because this setting affects how you learn a sport. And in turn, either helps you become the best player possible or works against you to limit your potential.

Formal and Informal Learning

Before we focus on sports, let's broaden our perspective. Consider for a moment how you collect knowledge about the world around you and learn everyday skills. Whenever you learn something new, you always do so in the context of a *learning environment.* This setting includes a physical or virtual location (classroom, gym, field, church, home, workplace, computer simulation, etc.). But more importantly, it's defined by *how you interact* with the person or thing doing the teaching. This relationship helps determine both what you learn and how well you learn it.

There are many different settings in which you learn. But they can usually be classified in one of two ways: formal (structured) or informal (unstructured). Both play an important part in your education.

Take, for example, how you learned to read.

You likely learned how to read at a public or private school. Lessons were given by a single teacher in a classroom filled with other students. What you learned was influenced by the quality of your teacher, the information taught, and possibly the number of students in the class. The teacher used a prescribed textbook and "class plan" to organize the information taught, and meet certain specified learning goals. This *formal* structured environment played a primary role in determining how well you learned to read.

But you may also have learned some rudimentary reading skills early-on through your parents' efforts at home. Your parents may have read to you when you were very young, prompted you to read along with them, and brought home books for you to read as you grew older. This more *informal* unstructured learning environment may have jump-started your interest in learning how to read. And as you learned how to read (and discovered you enjoyed it), you may have started to spend more of your free time reading on your own.

Importantly, this informal learning complemented your reading classes at school. At home you read different types of books including exciting adventure stories and fascinating biographies about famous people. You read at your own pace. Reading was fun. And because of this, you spent more time reading (and practicing your reading skills).

If you were exposed to both of the above learning environments in your early youth, you likely became a better reader who more thoroughly enjoyed reading.

Learning Environments in Sports

In learning how to play sports, you also do so in the context of different informal and formal learning environments. These include:

- Formal (Structured)

    o Organized youth sports

    o Competitive school or club sports

    o Personal trainers

- Informal (Unstructured)

    o Parental instruction

    o Pickup games

    o Practicing on your own

The formal learning environments (organized sports, school and club, and personal trainers) provide you with a top-down structured learning experience. They are similar to the classroom environment in our above reading example. They are led by an instructor (usually an adult) who controls the learning experience.

The informal learning environments (parental instruction, pickup games, and practicing on your own), on the other hand, are much less structured. Except for parental instruction, they are also self-directed. *You* determine with whom you play. *You* decide *how* you play (for fun or more serious competition). *You* decide what moves and techniques you will practice on your own and for how long.

Just as both formal and informal learning environments complemented each other in helping you learn how to read, they also do so in learning how to play sports. Each plays its part in providing you with a fuller understanding of how to play a sport well.

So let's now take a closer look at these learning environments and the specific benefits they provide you. We'll start by contrasting pickup games with "organized sports," discuss why you also need to practice on your own, and finally talk about blending these learning experiences together to get the most out of playing sports.

Pickup Games

Pickup games are ones that are organized and managed by the kids themselves—without help from adults. These are the neighborhood games played with friends in a backyard and the larger ones played among kids from different neighborhoods at a school, park, or community center.

These games are important. They help you get the most out of playing sports. Why? Because *playing and practicing sports in a self-directed setting provide you with possibly the best combination of fun and learning.*

The fun element is fairly obvious—you get to choose the type of game you enjoy playing. You and the other players decide whether your games are about relaxed fun or intense competition. It's up to you. With fun comes more participation, a natural desire to learn how to play better, great memories, and the long term health benefits of continued participation.

In their various formats, these pickup games also provide a fertile opportunity to learn your sport. Here are some of the ways in which playing pickup can help you learn how to play sports:

- *Informal instruction.* Older kids with whom you play pickup will know more than you and may be willing to teach you. If not, you can watch how they play the game and imitate their approach and technique. Eventually, you can test yourself against these more experienced players. Playing with friends who are younger or less skilled provides you with an opportunity to test your new "moves" in an environment where failure is less consequential.

- *Small-sided games.* Pickup games are often played with a smaller number of players than the required number for an "official" organized game. Fewer players (one-on-one, two-on-two, etc.) provide you with more "touches." More repetitions help you hone your skills.

- *Convenience.* The convenience of neighborhood games can result in more time spent practicing and learning your game. And with this additional investment of time, come the sports IQ and instincts that lead to success.

Besides helping you learn how to play a sport, pickup games also provide you with other personal benefits. Organizing and managing your own games helps develop your self-reliance. You learn how to persuade others to play, manage arguments, and find consensus within your group. These games also help you build social relationships with your friends (peer relationships), and in doing so, provide you with a strong sense of community.

As important as pickup games are to your development, they are unfortunately not what they once were. For better or worse, organized sports now play a greater role in the lives of today's kids.

> NOTE: For those of you who are new to playing sports,
> the next chapter covers pickup games in depth. This
> information will help you get the most out of playing
> pickup and provide you with a better understanding of
> the unwritten rules of pickup—ones that will help you
> blend in with other kids who enjoy playing sports.

Organized Sports

In past generations, pickup games dominated the youth sports scene. No longer—the world's changed.

You've got a lot more choices to entertain yourself including electronic games, smartphones, and cable TV. Life's more comfortable indoors with whole house air-conditioning. Today's parents are more concerned with safety. They're also busier. Both parents often work—and two-paycheck families mean fewer stay-at-home moms to supervise you and your friends. More so than the past, you live in a culture that views your personal development in terms of formal, scheduled activities (music and dance lessons, youth sports leagues, personal trainers). All of these factors have contributed to fewer pickup games.

Organized youth sports programs run by adults have instead taken over the typical child's sports life. Scheduled, highly structured, and safe, organized sports fit more easily into today's lifestyle.

Although these programs don't offer you the same benefits as pickup games, they do provide you with other essential benefits. Beyond the fundamental rewards of participating in sports (fun, fitness, community, etc.), these adult-run programs offer you:

- *Expert instruction.* Youth programs are often filled with dedicated, caring volunteer coaches who understand the sport they coach (and how to teach it).

- *Formal competition.* Practices and other goal-directed preparation, officials, coaches, a "clock," can all make for a more exciting competition.

- *A safe, structured learning environment.* Run by adults within a formal organization, most youth programs are geared first to your safety and development. These programs usually have established guidelines that help promote a fun learning environment.

- *Relationships with adults.* You gain experience interacting with adults, developing interpersonal skills that will benefit you later in life.

- *An opportunity to make new friends.* Organized sports often draw children together from different locations and backgrounds. This added diversity can help broaden your outlook on people and life.

For all the reasons mentioned above, playing organized sports is essential to your development.

If you enjoy sports and have a good coach and supportive parents, playing on a youth sports team should provide you with a great experience. Sure, there will be moments that challenge you—and possibly even scare you. It's normal to feel some nervousness and pressure when you're thrust into a new environment. But overall, the excitement of playing on an organized team, making new friends, and learning your sport should far surpass those fearful or disappointing moments.

Beware the Downside of Organized Sports

A mistake that you (or your parents) can make is to join too many organized programs and teams. If seasons overlap, then you may miss a team's practices and games, hurting your teammates' chances to succeed. Remember, youth sports are often *team* sports. Teammates have a responsibility to each other.

Another aspect of playing too many organized sports is that you increase the risk of "burning out" and killing your joy for playing. When practices become a chore, instead of something you look forward to, step back and look to see if you're spending too much time playing organized sports.

Finally, understand that *organized sports can crowd out the time you have available to play pickup games and practice on your own*. The unfortunate consequence is that you lose the unique and valuable benefits that are typically derived from the latter two types of play.

Balance Pickup Games, Organized Sports, and Practicing on Your Own

For most kids, a singular diet of organized sports run by adults is a mistake. You should instead seek a balance between organized sports, pickup games, and practicing on your own.

Here's a diagram that summarizes the benefits of both organized sports and self-directed play (pickup games).

Benefits of Self-Directed Play and Organized Sports

- *Peer relationships*
- *Self-determined fun*
- *Game management*
  (recruiting, arguments)
- *Self-reliance*

- *Expert instruction*
- *Formal competition*
- *Safety*
- *Adult relationships*
- *New, diverse friends*

| *Self-Directed Play* *(Pickup games)* | | *Organized Sports* *(Adult-run programs)* |

It's obvious that together, pickup games and organized sports provide greater benefits than either by itself.

But there's a third component to a balanced youth sports experience—*practicing on your own*. For you to maximize your playing potential, you *must* practice your individual skills. This activity is one that you will typically need to do on your own.

Organized sports and pickup games provide neither the opportunity nor the time to hone one's skills through the necessary practice repetitions. Yes, you may get some practice repetitions in these settings. These repetitions may be enough for you to understand how a skill is performed and how to do it during practice. But executing these skills at a high level in game situations requires that you react instinctively *without* conscious thought. This only occurs when you've conditioned your body and mind through hundreds (if not thousands) of repetitions.

Not only do practice repetitions bring instinctive execution of skills, they also breed another essential quality of excellent play— *confidence*. Having made thousands of practice free-throws, penalty shots, field goals, or pitches, you gain the self-assurance that your mind and body know how to perform a skill well. You believe you will succeed. When you take that pressure-filled shot at the end of the game, you fully expect it to go in. And more often than not, it does.

Practicing on your own also provides you the opportunity to explore variations of the skills you already know. Without any pressure, you can test these modified skills and decide whether they add value to your overall game.

In some sports, individual skills are more easily practiced on your own. Practicing a basketball shot on your driveway hoop is easier than figuring out a way to practice hitting a baseball in your backyard (or going to a batting cage). But in most sports, you can find different ways to practice essential skills.

A "wall" is often your friend for sports that use a ball. The wall can be a garage door, side of a building, or a fence. Using a wall, you can refine your tennis baseline groundstrokes, as well as net volley shots. If you're a pitcher, you can mark a batter's box on the wall with chalk and practice pitching to different spots. Baseball fielders can likewise throw a ball low against the wall and practice fielding the return ground ball. Soccer players can use a wall to help develop their ball control and kicking.

Finally, you can also team up with a friend to practice certain skills that are harder to practice on your own (throwing and catching a football, hitting a baseball).

With this practice component in mind, here's a diagram that represents the ideal balance in learning and playing sports:

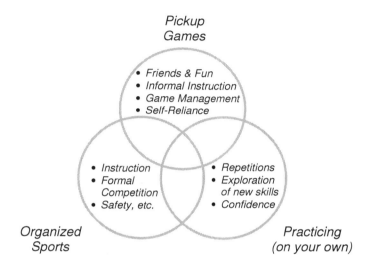

If you want to maximize your ability to play sports, and get the most out of your sports experience, you will need to invest time in all three components.

Now that you understand the different environments in which you learn how to play sports, let's move on and talk about specific learning approaches and techniques.

Playing Up, Playing Down

As touched upon earlier in this chapter, pickup games help you learn how to better play your sport. *Who* you play with impacts how and what you learn.

When you participate in a pickup game, *you* choose who you play with. Other kids can be just like you—the same age, same athletic ability, and same attitude about playing sports.

But you can also play with other kids who are either better or worse players than yourself. You can play with younger or older kids. You can play with kids who love sports or those who do so mainly to be part of the group.

Unlike adult-run organized sports, *you* are in control. And this provides you with the opportunity to tailor the games to exactly what you desire. Besides controlling the type of fun you want, you can also use pickup games as a means to practice skills and improve your game.

● Do not Play Up with a group of players that have skills *far better* than yours. If you're severely overmatched, these types of games won't help your development (and may hurt your confidence). Much better players will not want to play with you and they'll let you know it. If you're unsure whether you're a fit for a group of players, just hang around to see if you're asked to play. But be prepared for rejection!

You can pursue competitive play with older, more skilled athletes. This is referred to as *Playing Up*. This type of play provides you with an opportunity to test your skills against better players. You can see what works, what doesn't, and where you need to improve. You can observe how these more experienced kids play and possibly learn new skills. You may even find an older kid who will give you some advice and tips.

You also have a chance to learn different team roles. Against players who are the same age as you, you may be the star scorer. But against older kids, you will likely find yourself playing a more support-ive role (playing good defense, passing the ball, or setting screens for the more skilled players). Learning other roles is beneficial. It helps make you a well-rounded player that coaches will appreciate—an important asset when you reach a level of play where you're no longer the star player.

Playing Down is when you play sports with younger or less-skilled players. These may be the kids in your immediate neighborhood who are not especially athletic, but enjoy the communal aspect of playing sports with their friends. You may also find younger kids who love sports, aspire to be more like you, or just want to be included in the neighborhood group. In either setting, you become one of the better players.

Playing Down is important in two ways. First, it provides you with a more relaxed, fun environment in which to enjoy playing. You are less anxious about how well you perform and whether others will criticize your play. Secondly, when you're burned out from playing competitive organized sports, Playing Down with your friends can help rekindle your enjoyment for playing sports.

After a disappointing playoff loss that ended my senior year of high school basketball, I remember riding home on the team bus, staring out the window into the gray winter's night. Drained of emotion, the sense of emptiness I felt resembled the bleak, colorless world outside. At that moment, I could not have cared less about playing basketball. A part of me was relieved that the season was over.

A few days later, I decided to head over to a neighbor's driveway with my basketball. After shoveling off the snow, I began to shoot around. The repetition and rhythm, sensing my body flow through the cascades of movement, breathing in the cold air, and feeling the icy sting of the wet ball against my fingers, all seemed to act as a healing balm. A few other neighborhood friends showed up and we played some relaxed, fun games of two-on-two. When the games finally ended, I walked home— cold, wet and happy. I could feel my passion for playing the game returning.

▶ If you've just finished a long, hard season, take some time to relax. Decompress. Go out and just "shoot around." Play some catch with a friend. You'll feel your joy for playing the game quickly return.

Playing Down is also important in another way. It *provides you with an opportunity to develop and try out new skills*. Without any fear of criticism, you can experiment with different "moves." You can shoot the ball more, receive many more "touches," and see what it's like to play the role of the star player. Besides improving your skills, you also gain confidence—an important quality that leads to success in more competitive play. With added confidence that you can do something well, you're more motivated to practice and continue your development. All of which translates to even greater success against better competition.

Remember that different types of pickup games provide you with different benefits. By choosing who you play with, you also choose the benefits you want to pursue.

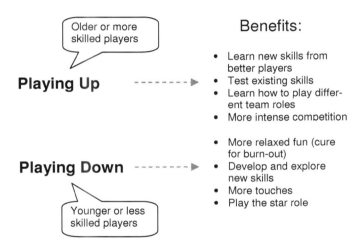

Older or more skilled players

Playing Up ‑ ‑ ‑ ‑ ‑ ‑ ‑ ▶

Playing Down ‑ ‑ ‑ ‑ ‑ ‑ ‑ ▶

Younger or less skilled players

Benefits:

- Learn new skills from better players
- Test existing skills
- Learn how to play different team roles
- More intense competition

- More relaxed fun (cure for burn-out)
- Develop and explore new skills
- More touches
- Play the star role

Take Advantage of Learning Resources

Years ago, kids learned how to play sports from parents, coaches, and other players. This is still the case. But unlike young athletes of the past, you also have an incredible selection of other instructional resources available to you.

Books like this one, along with hundreds of sports-specific ones, can help you better understand how to play and succeed in your sport.

You also have access to a large library of video instruction, much of it free. In any sport, you can buy instructional materials on DVD/Blu-ray discs or subscribe to similar online versions. Expanded coverage of sports on TV provides you with the opportunity to watch college and pro athletes play. If you watch these games as a student instead of a fan, you can pick up new, valuable skills. (In your personal practice time, emulate the way these players execute *fundamental* skills.)

▶ Many free instructional videos are available online (YouTube). Search for videos that are a good match for your age and skill level. (A young beginning basketball player does not need to learn advanced NBA moves!)

Another change from the past is the increased availability of personal coaches and trainers. For any sport, you can now find qualified local individuals who can (for an hourly fee) provide you with personalized instruction. This instruction typically focuses on either improving your sports skills or your physical conditioning and athleticism. There are even sports psychologists to help you with the mental aspects of your game. For those of you with the ability, interest, and financial resources, this instruction can raise your performance level.

▶ Books and online resources can also help beginners learn a sport's rules in a more comfortable setting. Although you may not yet know **how** to play, understanding the rules will give you one less thing to think about as you begin play.

Local clinics run by high school coaches can provide you with free instruction in a variety of team and individual sports. Overnight or week-long sports camps are available in most sports.

Although your parents may get you started in sports, it's up to you to take advantage of these resources. Don't be shy about asking others for tips on technique—many will gladly help you. Learn from your friends and peers. Soak up all the knowledge you can. Read books, online articles, and use video instruction to help you better understand and visualize specific techniques and moves.

💣These knowledge resources are worthless by themselves. You still need to translate this information to actual results. This means that you must practice, on your own, the techniques you learn.

To Learn Skills, Break Them Down

As you develop the necessary skills to play a sport, you will constantly need to learn new, more advanced ones. Some of these will come naturally, others will prove more difficult.

When you're struggling to learn a new skill, break it down into its fundamental components. Concentrate first on learning how to perform each part of the skill. *Then* begin to chain each element back together, adding one at a time. Depending on the skill (or how you best learn), focus initially on the first, last or most important part of the skill.

For example, young basketball players usually have difficulty shooting with their non-dominant hand. If you're right-handed, you may struggle trying to learn how to shoot a left-handed layup. You may be able to stand under the basket and bank the ball off the backboard into the basket using your left hand, but you just can't seem to dribble in, get your steps right, and then shoot the basketball.

In this example, you need to break down the layup into its primary skill components—the shot, your footwork, and the approach dribble. Start with the shot itself. You want to use your outside left hand to shoot the basketball with your inside right foot on the floor (and left knee up). Practice this

46

element until you feel comfortable shooting off of your right foot and can consistently make the shot. Now, introduce the footwork. Stand approximately two steps back and walk through the approach while saying "Left, Right, Shoot." Try to establish and feel a natural rhythm to these connected movements.

Once you're comfortable shooting a left-handed layup with these steps, it's time to add dribbling. Move an extra step further away. Dribble once with your left hand (with your right foot contacting the floor as the ball bounces), take your two steps (Left, Right), and then, with your right foot planted, take your layup shot (Shoot). Finally, when you're ready, move further back and add more dribbles.

Practice the complete skill. You will struggle with this for a while, but your mind will start to subconsciously understand your distance from the hoop and shorten or extend your steps to compensate.

Think of how you can apply this approach to your sport. Here's another quick example. If you're learning how to shoot a soccer ball with power, break down the skill into its three basic components (1) the approach step and foot plant (leg back), (2) the position of your leg and foot (with ankle locked, toe down) as you're about to strike the ball, and (3) your follow-through and landing (on the same foot you kicked with). Try doing an abbreviated one-step approach sequence, first without a ball and then with a ball. Finally, add a full, running approach (without stutter steps).

By breaking down a skill into its component parts, practicing each part, and then practicing the entire sequence, you will more quickly master the skill.

Learning a new skill

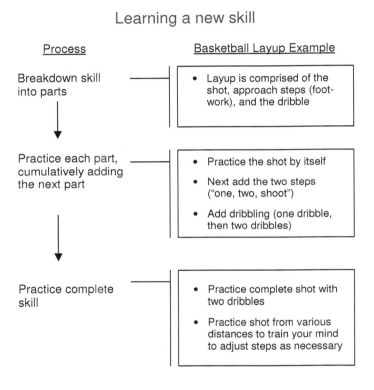

Process	Basketball Layup Example
Breakdown skill into parts	• Layup is comprised of the shot, approach steps (footwork), and the dribble
Practice each part, cumulatively adding the next part	• Practice the shot by itself • Next add the two steps ("one, two, shoot") • Add dribbling (one dribble, then two dribbles)
Practice complete skill	• Practice complete shot with two dribbles • Practice shot from various distances to train your mind to adjust steps as necessary

Do It the Same Way Every Time

Many factors determine your success in executing a sports skill including your natural athleticism, technique, and your body's physical condition. However, some skills depend to a large degree on practice and repetition—and *performing the skill the same way every time*. With thousands of identical practice repetitions, these sports skills become ingrained (*muscle memory*). And importantly, they hold up in stressful, pressure-packed moments.

For instance, let's take a look at free throw shooting in basketball. Like any other shot, the free throw benefits from proper technique. But this shot is different from others in that it's attempted from the same position on the court each time without an opponent trying to block the shot. Although helpful, athleticism (good hand-eye coordination, strength, etc.) is less important than other shots. If your technique is reasonably good, your ability to convert a high percentage of your shots will largely depend on how often you practice free throws. Performing these practice shots over and over the same way (and doing so when tired) will help you establish the muscle memory necessary to lock-in a repeatable motion—one that will work even in difficult game situations.

▶ When developing new skills, you will likely experiment with different variations of technique. But once you have established the form and technique that works best for you, it is essential that you practice the skill the same way every time.

Other sports have similar specialized shots that greatly benefit from practice repetitions. Examples include kicking a field goal in football, pitching in baseball, and shooting a penalty shot in hockey or soccer.

Excellence in these types of sports skills provides you with yet another opportunity to successfully compete against a more athletic opponent.

But Also Push the Edges of Your Game

As discussed above, success in sports depends not only on talent but also on preparation and practice. Practice takes individual talent to the next level, honing your skills through repetition.

Although fundamental skills are necessary to play any sport well, and essential to developing more advanced skills, be careful not to limit the possibilities of your game. Doing the same thing, the same

💣⚡Although practice repetitions are necessary to improve and lock-in a skill, refining a mediocre technique only takes you so far. Pay attention to *what* you practice. Search for better techniques, the ones that can dramatically improve your game.

way, over and over, not only gets boring but also can limit your sense of the possible and constrain your ability.

To better enjoy your sport and become more proficient, you sometimes need to break out and try new ideas, physical movements, and skill techniques. You need to practice at the edge of your abilities and beyond. Although you will fail more often outside your comfort zone, and possibly become frustrated with your mistakes, this experience is a necessary part of the learning process. It's the stage that primes your leap to a higher level of performance. Instead of refining a skill to incrementally improve, you elevate that skill in a way that provides you with a new competitive advantage.

For example, you may have an excellent stationary shot in basketball or soccer. But can you take and make that shot while on the move or when defended? You can practice your stationary shot over-and-over, but if you can't get it off in a game, it's not of much use. For the basketball player, it may not be enough to refine his or her outside "set" shot. Learning how to shoot a pull-up jumper off the dribble may instead be the approach that makes that player's game more effective.

Let your imagination flow

Ideally, your game is grounded in the fundamentals—but is not mechanical; you are able to spontaneously and creatively react to novel game situations. Sometimes real game situations require you to spontaneously adapt. If you occasionally practice body-twisting impossible shots, moves, or catches, you will both have fun and gain body control for those unplanned moments in your sport.

Set aside a few minutes in your personal practices to have fun. For example, in basketball, practice spontaneous, inventive, wild shots on occasion. Pretend you're in a dunking contest and perform a 360-degree move on your way to the hoop. Shoot that hook shot from half-court. Let your imagination go and conceive a totally new shot or dribbling move—try it out!

Who knows, *you* may be the one who needs to sink that half court shot with time running out!

💣*Trying to do too much in a game, and pushing yourself beyond your actual ability, will usually result in too many errors. To maximize your performance, rely on proven skills— play within yourself.

Practice in Game-like Conditions

It's not enough to simply learn how to execute sports skills. Learning how to shoot with the proper form is only part of learning how to score. You must also learn how to perform these skills in games. To do so, you need to practice your skills in conditions that more closely duplicate the ones you will face in games.

What are game-like conditions?

Let's look at the skill of shooting a ball or puck. Besides executing the mechanics of the skill itself, here are some additional factors that affect your performance:

- *Defense.* In games you have an opponent actively trying to block or otherwise affect your shot. You must learn how to get your shot off while defended. To do so, you must be able to momentarily free yourself from your defender ("create space"). You may also need to adjust your shot, sometimes taking it off-balance or from less than ideal body positions. Shots are taken not just from stationary positions, but also on the move.

- *Fatigue.* In games you will take shots when you're tired or out-of-breath. You will sometimes need to adjust your shot to compensate for muscle fatigue. You must learn to focus and

51

gather your energy even as fatigue is weakening your body and willpower.

- *Pressure.* Besides defensive pressure, you will also face mental pressure. Whether it's a last second shot to win the game or making a wide open shot in front of many fans, you face the challenge of maintaining your concentration. You must live in the moment and not think "what if." Even the best professionals feel this kind of pressure.

So how do you better handle the types of pressures highlighted above? You simulate these conditions in your shooting drills and pickup games.

Instead of simply practicing a shot over and over in a relaxed way, introduce a competitive element. In basketball, for example, see how many free throws you can make in a row. Play games like "Around-the-World" against a friend where you go back to the beginning if you miss a shot two times in a row. While practicing, imagine that you've got the ball in your hands with the clock ticking down. You need to make that last second shot to win the game. 3-2-1…

All of the above introduce mental pressure. What about fatigue? Use drills that require movement prior to the shot and continuous repetition. These will gradually fatigue your body and create a more game-like condition. Practice some of your shots when you're already tired. In a basketball game, you're often trying to catch your breath when you go to the line to shoot free throws. So duplicate the game situation. Practice your free throws immediately after you've played or finished a taxing drill.

> ▶ Besides using repetitions to lock in a skill's technique, also practice variations. Execute the skill from different locations on the court or field. By mixing up the conditions, you learn in a way that will transfer over to your performance in a game.

To learn how to handle defensive pressure, you need to play against an opponent. By playing pickup and other small-sided games (one-on-one, two-on-two) you get more touches and more opportunity to learn what works and what doesn't. Through repetition, you gain experience. And with added experience, your mind better recognizes when to take that shot and how to get it off.

To practice more effectively, make sure that you balance all of the above practice elements. Complement practicing your "form" with other drills and activities that add game-like conditions. Remember, your ultimate goal isn't to make ten shots in a row from the same spot on your driveway. It's to make that shot in a game.

Learn New Skills and Correct Deficiencies in the Off-Season

A coach will usually match a player's physical abilities and skill set to a position or role on a team. This is a normal and understandable process. Your coach is trying to maximize the team's chance to win with the players at hand. Your coach is also trying to provide *you* with the best individual opportunity to succeed. But you should also realize that this does not mean that you're forever locked into any one role.

Although you may *now* play your game with limited ability and success, most young athletes will naturally undergo major physical changes and an accompanying improvement in their skills. Although you have little control over your height and body type, you can work to improve your skills.

You can sometimes improve your skills during your current sport season; however, be careful not to experiment with changes that either hurt your performance or reduce your confidence. A better approach is to tackle any major changes in the off-season. This is when you have the time and unpressured opportunity to learn a new shot, add a fresh move, and correct skill deficiencies.

One of my most memorable sports success stories came while playing Pony League baseball. Although I was a successful pitcher in Little League, my only strength was good control—I possessed neither a real fastball nor curveball. On my freshman high school team I could not compete as a pitcher and instead played other fielding positions (without much success). I was the weakest player on the team and saw little playing time in games.

At the end of the season, I asked one of our pitchers how he threw his curveball. It was a good one, with lots of break. He showed me how he tucked his index finger in and against the ball to make it easier to generate spin. I took this advice and experimented with a sponge rubber baseball, throwing it against the brick wall between my house's garage doors. I became excited when I saw my ball breaking and realized that I was able to throw a curveball (actually a knuckle curve).

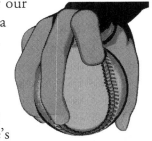

Because of the increased stress on your elbow ligaments, many experts recommend that you don't begin throwing a curveball until you are at least 14 years old. Also, limit your "pitch count" when practicing.

I found some chalk, drew a batter's box on the brick and stepped off the distance on my driveway back to the "pitcher's rubber." I spent the next three weeks practicing, throwing my new curveball from different positions (overhand, sidearm), and developing my control of this pitch to the point that I could consistently hit any spot in the batter's box.

When my Pony League season started, I found myself on a good team, but one without any exceptional pitchers. I quickly became the "ace" of our staff and dominated the teams I pitched against. My team won most of our games and we ended our season in first place.

Especially satisfying were the two games I pitched against a team comprised mainly of boys from my freshmen baseball team. I won both games, throwing a two-hit shutout in the first game and a five-hit win in the second one. I went on to pitch in our league's all-star game and won our team's MVP award.

Who would have thought that the worst kid on his freshman baseball team would enjoy this level of success just two months later? In my case, learning one new skill made the difference.

Always search for new techniques that can change your game for the better. Practice hard and know that it's possible for you to find different roles and learn new skills that can lead to personal success.

> ▶ When it comes to learning how to perform a skill, don't be shy. Always ask more talented players for their advice. More often than not they will help you.

Over-Exaggerate Skill Elements to Correct Form

When learning a new skill, you will likely struggle to perform it well. You may be overwhelmed with the "mechanics" of a technique and initially unable to absorb and integrate the multiple elements that comprise the skill. Breaking down a skill into its fundamental parts, practicing each part, and then chaining them together, will help you with this process.

More experienced players may encounter a different skill-related problem. In learning a new skill, they may have developed improper techniques—and locked themselves into habits that are incorrect and inefficient. In these instances, a player's mind ("muscle memory") continues to stubbornly execute an element of the skill in a manner that either understates or overstates the proper position, motion, or timing.

To correct a stubborn deficiency in your form, briefly over-exaggerate the skill element in the same or opposite direction. For example, if your basketball shot is too flat, practice shooting the ball with a higher release point and a much greater arc (same direction). If you continuously slice a golf ball with an outside-inside swing, you might temporarily use a more closed stance to generate a hook (opposite direction).

Correcting a shot that is too flat

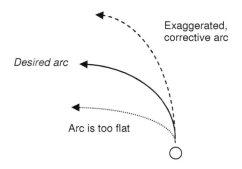

Exaggerated, corrective arc

Desired arc

Arc is too flat

Ray Searage, the Pittsburgh Pirates pitching coach, recently helped one of his pitchers change his throwing motion. Charlie Morton, a pitcher with outstanding "stuff," unfortunately could not translate his ability into success on the field. He suffered a horrendous 2010 season (2-12; 7.57 ERA).

💣 Be careful with this approach—you do not want to substitute one bad habit for another. Also, before resorting to this learning technique, first make sure that there is not an obvious deficiency (e.g., incorrect grip) that you can easily correct.

After analyzing video, Searage noticed that Charlie's overhand throwing motion seemed unnatural and forced. As Searage said, "Everything we saw went back to Charlie being something he wasn't." He decided to have Charlie try throwing with a three-quarters delivery. How did he introduce this new motion to Charlie?

At the beginning of a long-pitch session, he shouted, "Hey, Chuck, just throw sidearm!" As Searage explained, "You tell somebody who throws over the top to throw sidearm, and he'll go three-quarters." Coupled with a revised grip on his sinker pitch, Charlie Morton's modified delivery yielded excellent results throughout the 2011 baseball season. [3]

If you're like Charlie Morton, your new form may immediately feel natural. Simply practicing the revised skill will lock it in.

For others, the exaggerated form will feel awkward. That's not necessarily bad. It means that your mind is experiencing new neural connections—you're starting to break an ingrained habit.

As this process continues, slowly back off the exaggerated technique to achieve the proper form. You can then lock it in through practice and repetition. Whenever you feel that you are reverting to your older, incorrect form, go through this process and over-exaggerate the skill in question.

Don't Forget the Fundamentals

As you get older and your skills improve, your game will become more complete. You will become bigger, faster, and stronger. You'll perform at a higher level and execute more complex skills. But as your game expands, it's important that you don't lose sight of your fundamental skills.

During each practice (at the beginning or end) spend several minutes executing your essential shots or other skills, concentrating on your form. Do this in a way that you are not challenged by the physical characteristics of the skill such as speed, quickness or strength. Execute the skill with a comfortable, even tempo. Move closer to the goal if you're shooting or throwing a ball. As you flow through each element of the skill, *feel* whether your movements match your mental picture of the respective element that belongs to the *perfect* shot or other skill. Repeat this multiple times until you have executed the skill with perfect form—*then* move back to your normal distance (if you're shooting or throwing) and bring up the skill's execution speed to its typical level.

💣In your haste to add more skills, don't lose the ones you already have! Regularly return to and practice the essential, basic skills of your sport to keep the foundation of your game strong.

For example, in basketball, take a few minutes practicing your shooting motion three to five feet in front of the basketball hoop.

Focus on a perfect grip and arm setup (form an "L" and pretend you're carrying a pizza above your head). Place your non-shooting hand to your side or behind your back. Use your legs to push the "L" upward into a smooth release that generates backspin and a high arc. Follow-through with your hand extended over and into the basket.

In tennis, you might start your practice by hitting easy groundstrokes with your partner *from the service line*, concentrating on good form (emphasizing a fluid motion with topspin). Every sport has its essential skills that you can practice in this manner.

Whenever you feel your form deteriorating while practicing a normal shot or skill, stop and perform the actions described above. Your goal in practice is to develop repeatable skill movements, ones that incorporate the form that will most consistently give you the best result. Do not reinforce bad form by poor practice habits! With few exceptions, you're as good as your practice.

Participate in Multiple Sports

As you progress through youth sports, both your sports skills and interest in playing sports will evolve. Most likely, one sport will emerge as your favorite, while others, although enjoyable, will fill a different secondary role.

In some situations, your parents or coaches may push you to concentrate on a single sport—sometimes at an early age. More talented athletes are often identified early and funneled into lessons and competitive leagues that dominate their young athletic lives. The idea, of course, is to quickly develop advanced skills and maximize the young athlete's potential. This approach is often taken by parents who see their children as potential prodigies in individual sports such as tennis or gymnastics. In competitive youth team sports, Amateur Athletic Union (AAU) and club teams often pull a child into a single sport mode.

Unfortunately, there are several drawbacks with this path. You potentially lose out on the many benefits that come from playing multiple sports. Let's take a look at some of these.

> ▶ As you age and your focus tightens, continue to participate in multiple sports for both the crossover and enjoyment benefits. At a smaller high school, you may enjoy the opportunity to play in multiple varsity sports. You may also find that your "secondary" sport is your best sport.

Skill crossover

As you develop specific advanced skills in one sport, you may miss out on the crossover benefits that are generated by playing other sports. Each sport has its own set of skills and effect on an athlete's body, and sometimes these provide an athlete with an advantage in another sport.

For instance, an athlete's improved movement and footwork gained by playing tennis may translate into an unexpected advantage when the athlete plays soccer. Strategic and tactical skills often cross over from one sport to another (and may help an athlete take a more creative approach within their primary sport). A "give and go" two-man play in basketball is much the same as it is in soccer, hockey, and other team sports. Likewise, hand-eye coordination, often translates from one sport to another. A tennis overhead and serve requires the same hand-eye coordination skills as those used to spike and serve a volleyball.

Each sport uses your muscles and joints differently. Sometimes the physical aspect of one sport can complement others, and help improve performance in these other sports. For example, if you participate in a summer youth swimming program you may become stronger—and find that this added strength benefits your performance in other sports.

💣✷We live in a more sports-specific world than years ago and high school coaches have more latitude in running off-season activities. Many coaches frown on their players participating in other sports—and not always for the right reasons. You may face pressure from one or more of your coaches to concentrate on *their* sport. Before you go down this path, make sure it's really *your* sport. Don't unnecessarily sacrifice the rewards of participating in multiple sports.

More fun, great memories, less injuries, and new friends

Playing several sports also safeguards your health. Participating in different physical activities helps avoid overuse and excessive strain on particular muscles and joints.

In addition to the crossover skill and physical benefits, participating in other sports can provide you with a more relaxed form of *competitive fun*. This, in turn, can prevent you from burning out in your primary sport.

Secondary sports can also provide you with great sports experiences that create memorable, satisfying moments. Although I played three years of varsity tennis in high school, this sport was less important to me than basketball. Nevertheless, tennis provided me with several memorable moments. The most satisfying "comeback" of my personal sports life occurred in a sectional first-doubles match. Down a set to a talented (and arrogant) doubles team, my partner and I gathered ourselves and went on to take the match from our surprised and frustrated opponents.

You can meet new and interesting friends when you play multiple sports. To get in shape for my senior year of high school basketball, I decided to go out for cross-country. I wasn't one of our team's better runners (we won the New York State championship that year), but I still ran competitive times when compared to the runners on other teams. Practices and races were difficult, and I probably did improve my overall endurance. But the most rewarding benefit was the friendships I established—especially with one of the guys on the team. Some of my best memories of that final year in high school are associated with the "adventures" we shared.

Select sports in which you can succeed

Finally, when choosing your sports in high school, consider not only your desire to play a sport but also your potential for success. Ideally, you want to select those sports you both enjoy and can play well. (The former sometimes depends on the latter.) Be careful not to be misled by your friends.

I almost chose track (high jumping) instead of tennis during the spring of my senior year in high school. I got caught up in some sales pitches given to me by my track and cross-country buddies. Luckily, I

> ▶ Select the sports that are right for you, not your friends!

received some good advice from our school's athletic director. He pointed out to me that, although I might become an average high jumper, my potential for success in tennis was much greater. As it turned out, my regular season record was 10-1 playing second singles and I played in our section's doubles championship match. It's unlikely I would have had near that success as a track high jumper.

Don't shortchange yourself. Play as many sports as you can when you're young. You'll make new friends, help protect yourself from injury and burnout, enjoy crossover benefits, gain a better understanding of which sports you really enjoy, and ultimately, have more fun and success!

Off to Camp

If you truly enjoy playing sports, consider attending a sports camp. These camps typically are offered for each sport and organized either in a day or overnight format, running from a couple of days to one or more weeks. Multi-sport camps are also available as well as position-specific sports camps.

Before attending a sports camp, first take advantage of local clinics. These half or full-day instructional sessions are usually organized and run by your town, high school coach, or local club. Low cost (or free) clinics provide a great opportunity for you to learn fundamental skills and techniques. When run by your high school's coach, the clinics expose you to the concepts and skills most valued by the coach. They also enable the coach to better appreciate your skills and talent.

A sports camp can provide you with several benefits including: quality instruction, physical conditioning, competition, and the opportunity to make new friends.

●⁎Some paid camps are huge money makers for schools, coaches, and sports stars. If a camp emphasizes playing games over teaching skills, the primary gains for you are likely a free tee shirt, a ball, a cap, or anything that advertises the camp.

If you want to "live and breathe" your sport, overnight week-long camps immerse you in the ultimate sports and social experience. Sleeping and eating together, learning and competing, each athlete is thrown into an exciting world that revolves entirely around their passion. New friends are made, self-reliance developed, and more advanced individual and team sports skills are learned. You can walk away from these camps with a fresh perspective on both your sport and your life.

But also understand that these camps rarely make you an overnight sensation. Don't expect that a week of camp instruction will transform you into a star player.

For older, more competitive athletes, "showcase" camps are also available. In addition to instruction and competition, these camps (popular in baseball, basketball and football) are often attended by college coaches. They can provide you with an opportunity to gain exposure and *possibly* help you secure a college scholarship.

💣 Do not select a camp based on the star athletes who are attending the camp or acting as camp counselors. Similar to other educational settings, the most talented performer is not necessarily the best teacher.

When selecting a camp, try to locate one whose mission is closely aligned with your needs. Understand the camp's philosophy and goals, the schedule of a typical day, and the camper to counselor ratio. Look for camps that have instructors and counselors who can provide you with the best developmental experience.

To locate the best sports camp, consult with your local high school coach and check online resources (i.e., camp organizations). Contact your local colleges to determine what camps they offer. Also, ask other kids who play the same sport about their personal experience with camps.

A Primer on
Pickup Games

*When I play basketball at the YMCA, I feel
like some of the guys don't want me on
their team. Can you offer any advice on how
to fit in better?*

... Matt

Pickup games are a great way to both have fun and learn how to play a sport. If you have older brothers and sisters, or friends who enjoy sports, you probably already know something about playing pickup. But if you're new to sports, you may be a little confused about these games. And if you're not as naturally athletic as some of your friends, or somewhat shy, you also may be struggling to fit in.

This chapter will help you understand the basics of playing pickup—how to organize a game, choose teams, and manage the play. You will learn more about *why* you should play pickup. And finally, you will discover the types of behavior that determine whether or not you're accepted by your fellow players.

What Makes Pickup Unique?

Many of you have probably played in an organized sports program. Your parents signed you up, you were placed on a team with a coach, and you played scheduled games officiated by referees.

Most of you have probably also played in at least a few neighborhood games of touch football, soccer, basketball, baseball, or hockey. (If not, consider the other casual games you've played with kids in your neighborhood.) If you think back to those early neighborhood games, something was very different about them. *Unlike organized sports, there were no adults to pick the teams, decide on the rules, or manage arguments.* In addition, each one of you could decide to play or not play. You and your friends were in total control of the experience—you owned the game.

Because you and your friends are in charge of these games, you have the freedom to participate in the type of play *you* want (or need). You can explore playing sports in different ways. And as a result, pickup games provide you with several benefits not typically found in the other types of sports activities organized and run by adults.

Why You Should Play Pickup

Pickup games represent what's best in sports—playing for fun, competing in the purest sense, and sharing a rewarding experience with others. There's no money, no cheerleaders, and no trophies—none of the external rewards that sometimes accompany organized sports.

But watch any group of friends playing a game of pickup. Athletic *or not*, each of the players is having fun, enjoying both the play and each other's company. In the more competitive pickup games, players are expending every ounce of energy seeking to play their best and help their team win. They compete for the fun of it.

Pickup games provide something for everyone. They complement organized sports, providing you with a different set of benefits. Sometimes they are the remedy for *too* many organized sports practices and games. Pickup games develop your sports skills, but in a way that supplements the instruction and drills found in organized sports.

Organizing and managing your own pickup games also helps develop your self-reliance. And most importantly, they let you get the type of fun out of sports that *you* need.

So with these general benefits in mind, let's explore the types of pickup games you can play, how to join in on the fun, and how to improve your game by playing pickup.

Types of Pickup Games

If you regularly play pickup, you already understand how these games can change, depending on who is playing. But for those new to pickup, let's take a closer look at the nature of these games.

Typically, pickup games fall into one of the following three categories:

1. *Backyard, driveway, or street games with 2 to 10 players, most of whom are from the immediate neighborhood.* Games can be relaxed fun with modified rules, or more structured and competitive. Games usually include players of different ages and abilities.

2. *Games that draw from multiple local streets or neighborhoods, and are played at a school, park, or community center.* These games are often competitive and typically have more formal rules agreed to before the game. These games may include kids who do not know each other well. These games are organized through pre-game communication among players.

3. *Games that are played at a specific time and place (local YMCA, park, school) and don't require any pre-game communications.* Players show up and teams are picked based on the standing rules specific to that court or field. Games are competitive and comprised of skilled players of various ages.

▶ Games that involve strangers or kids from other neighborhoods are typically more structured. Depending on the mix of players, they also may be more competitive than the ones you play with your neighborhood friends. Besides the formal rules, there are informal ones that govern acceptable behavior (e.g., what is considered a foul). Be prepared to quickly learn the group's rules and accordingly adapt your play.

Of course, there are variations of the above. For example, similar to number 3 above, a group of kids may arrive at their local YMCA after school lets out. But depending on who shows up, their skill level and age, the games may either be relaxed fun or more competitive and serious.

Always keep in mind that the unique aspect of pickup games is that they are totally under the control of you and the other players. This is especially true of the games you play with your friends and neighbors. If everyone wants to play a pickup game of basketball wearing roller skates, then do it. It's about having *fun*— in whatever way you and your friends define it.

Organizing a Game

Unlike adult-run "organized sports," you and your friends are responsible for putting together your game. No adult help is needed.

Years ago, neighborhood games in the summer were set up by calling your friends on the phone or knocking on doors. If you were in school, you might pass the word to your friends when and where the game would occur.

Some of the old communication methods still apply today. Word of mouth, phone calls, and knocking on a door or two are still ways to get the word out and gather players. But kids today have even more tools to easily organize their games. Almost everyone over 13 years of age has a cell phone and the ability to "text" others. Facebook and other social networking web sites provide a central point to post plans for a pickup game. There are even web sites specifically designed to help you put together a pickup game in your neighborhood or town.

When organizing your game, you need to select the right location. Why? Because a game's setting sometimes affects the game itself. Too large a field for the number of players can result in too much scoring, running, and a game that ends quickly. Too many players for a small field can diminish the game's flow and opportunity to make plays.

To help ensure an enjoyable, long-lasting game, select a place to play that matches the type of game and the number of available players. A backyard is convenient and cozy for a small friendly game of touch football or stickball/whiffleball. A driveway is good for small basketball games (1-on-1, 2-on-2, 3-on-3). For larger games, a field at a local school or park is the right choice. These more "official" fields impart a greater sense of importance to your game.

Sometimes you don't need to organize small neighborhood games—they spontaneously happen. You may be shooting baskets in a driveway, and other kids see you and decide to join in. What starts out as "shooting around" evolves into a game of 1-on-1, 2-on-2, or 3-on-3.

Similar to a driveway game of 2-on-2 that no one specifically organizes, larger games often arise at your local park, playground, school, or YMCA. In this setting, it becomes common knowledge that players will regularly show up on a certain day and time. Without any one individual having to organize these games, they will continue—as long as a minimum

▶ Do you like organizing events? If so, you can play an important role in helping make the game happen. This is one way for a less athletic kid to gain acceptance within the community of kids who play together.

▶ If someone just moved into your neighborhood, pickup games are an excellent icebreaker to help you and your friends meet the new boy or girl. All it takes is one person to go knock on the door and ask whether the new kid is interested in playing some ball.

number of players consistently show up. But when kids begin to lose interest and momentum is lost, the games will end. So if you want to keep these regular games going, you may occasionally need to promote them to your friends.

Picking Teams

You've organized the time and place for your game. Everyone has arrived. Now you need to pick teams.

There are several ways to go about this and each group of kids usually has its own way of selecting teams.

First players to make a shot

In certain sports, some kids find it easiest to select teams of players based on who is the first to make a shot or goal. In basketball, for example, players line up and take turns shooting a free throw. The first five to make the shot are the ones who comprise the first team. If there are more than ten players, the second team is comprised of the next five to make the shot. For the last team, multiple elimination rounds may be necessary (where it's agreed that each player gets at least one shot and more than five players make their shot).

The advantage of this approach is that it takes "politics" out of the selection process. Players are selected based on their performance—not on friendships or who knows who. No one is picked last. The disadvantage of this selection process is that it can generate teams that are unbalanced, resulting in a one-sided game that isn't fun. It can also take longer to select teams using this method.

▶ If one team is clearly weaker than another, you may want to voice your concern. In less competitive settings, teams will trade players to create more equal teams and a better game.

Using captains

Another way to choose teams is for two or more players to act as "captains." These individuals are often the best players (but not always). What's important is that the captains are close in playing ability and know the abilities of the other kids. The goal in most neighborhood pickup games is to select two teams that are relatively equal. Everyone wants a good game where each team has an opportunity to win.

If you're a captain, carefully evaluate the available players. Try to select not only the best players, but ones who can play the key positions necessary to compete. In basketball, for instance, you would look to pick both a point guard and big man (at least one of whom is a scorer). In a game of football, each team needs a quarterback who can throw a football reasonably well.

Understand that this selection process is often influenced by social factors (friendships, class, personalities). Sometimes the captains are the kids with the most power in the group—and their first choices made based on friendships rather than ability. Politics are part of life, and sports mirror life in many ways. If you are offended by being picked behind players with less ability, use this emotion to fuel your performance. Over the long run, superior ability usually trumps non-performance factors.

In what order do captains pick? Captains will typically either take sequential turns (1-2-3, 1-2-3, etc.) or use a reversing "Snake" format (1-2-3, 3-2-1, etc.). The Snake method (see diagram) is best when you're choosing more than two teams. It also helps balance teams when there is a major drop-off in talent from the begin-

💣 In more competitive settings, where "winners stay on" the court or field, captains will more aggressively pursue "stacking" their team with the best players possible.

💣 If you're a captain in a competitive game, pick well! Otherwise, you will lose the respect of your fellow players. Remember that players want to win (to possibly stay on and play more). You need good players at key positions to have a chance to compete!

ning of a round to its end (i.e., the first player is much better than the second and third player available).

Picking Teams using Snake Format

Captain 1	Captain 2	Captain 3
Round 1		
"Star" Player	Excellent Player	Very Good Player
Round 2		
Good Player	Good Player	Very Good Player
Round 3		
Fair Player	Fair Player	Fair Player

Which of the captains pick first? There are many ways to determine this, depending on the sport. In a baseball game, one captain can toss a bat toward the other captain who then grabs it towards the bottom. Each captain takes turns putting his or her hand above the other's one, until no room is left. The last captain with his hand fully on the bat picks first. In a basketball game, the two captains often shoot free throws or three point shots—with the first one to miss becoming the second captain to pick. You can also flip an object (coin), play odds and evens with your fingers ("1-2-3-Shoot!", "Let's shoot for it"), or play "Rock, Paper, Scissors."

Sign-up lists and "Who has winners?"

If you're showing up to play in a regularly scheduled game, teams are usually selected on a "first come, first serve" basis. The first players to arrive, up to the total needed to begin the game, are the ones who get to play first. Any other players who came after this first group must wait to play the next game (or possibly the ones afterward).

Sometimes there's a sign-up list to help clarify the order of who arrived first. In other settings, it's simply word of mouth among the waiting players "who has next." It's up to you to make sure that both you and the other players know where you are in this pecking order. In a familiar setting, don't be shy when you arrive. Speak-up! You must assert yourself to make sure that others know you're waiting to play and where you are in the queue of waiting players. This will help preempt any potential confusion or arguments.

You may occasionally find yourself in a dispute about who showed up first. The more competitive the games are, the more likely this will occur.

Understand that who gets to play next is not *always* about fairness—it's sometimes political. In playground games involving tight groups of friends, players will sometimes exercise their power within the group. Player "privileges" in these settings can prevail over fairness.

You will need to decide how strongly you feel about your right to play and whether it's worth a potential argument. Sometimes it's like a game of poker. Others will try to bluff that they arrived before you. You can either raise the stakes or fold your cards.

💣 When several teams are waiting to play in a winners stay-on setting, it's more likely that other kids will fudge the rules. Some players will want to play with the better players or their friends. Watch any sign-up list to ensure no one erases your name or that players on the list are actually waiting (and not already playing). Talk with others to make sure they know when you showed up and which waiting team you are playing. If there is a dispute, they will often come to your defense.

While you're waiting to play, you may recognize a potential dispute—some other players acting as if they're "on" next. If you're not sure of your position (and the support you will get from others waiting), do not force the issue before the current game ends. Instead, after the game ends, immediately walk onto the court or field and confidently act as though you're part of the waiting team. Depending on how strongly the other players react, you can then accordingly defend your claim.

When you're in the right, stubbornly persevering will often cause others to back down (especially in semi-supervised settings such as a

YMCA). In some situations, you may decide that it's simply not worth the effort to defend your position. You can instead choose to wait for the next game; saying loudly so everyone hears, "I've got winners." You can also walk away and find another pickup game elsewhere.

Playing with a Group for the First Time

Although many of your pickup games are with friends, there are times when you will play with a new group of kids, most of whom you don't know.

This can be intimidating, especially if you're playing with older kids or better players.

If you're asked to play by someone you know, then your friend will probably introduce you to some of the other players. Watch how your friend interacts with the other kids and follow along.

> ▶ Find out what time regularly scheduled pickup games start, and arrive early. While warming-up, you'll have a chance to meet other players and discover how the games are run.

If you're showing up for the first time at a place that has regularly scheduled pickup games, then you will need to find out how to get into a game. Since you're a stranger (and not necessarily needed for the game to go on), it's your responsibility to approach someone in the group. Pick someone who looks friendly and ask them, "Who has winners?" If that group has some special way of selecting who plays when, that person will let you know.

Remember: each group of players has its own rules. You may need to sign-up on a sheet of paper, find out which team has "next" and whether they need a player, or possibly (in basketball) shoot free throws to see who plays.

The easiest way to blend in is to quietly demonstrate to the other kids your ability. Better athletes will quickly be accepted on the merit of their ability, while lesser athletes will find acceptance by their willingness to initially play smaller roles. Once you get to know the other players, you can let more of your personality shine.

If you're playing with older players, it's even more important to initially take a low-key approach to playing. They may want you around only if they lack enough players to play the game. Be humble. As you show some athleticism or willingness to play a supporting role (e.g., play tough defense, make good passes), it's likely they will accept you.

Advice for the Novice

Pickup games are fun partly because you get to play with your friends and be part of the group. Especially in neighborhood games, there's a wide mix of kids of different ages and athletic ability. Just because you're younger or not one of the better players doesn't mean you can't join in on the fun! Here's an approach that will help you play more effectively and gain acceptance.

💣 It's usually a mistake to try and bluff others about your ability or knowledge of the game. More often, you will expose your lack of experience. Other players will immediately assume you lack skill (and an understanding of your limitations), and will avoid playing with you.

In talking above about playing with a group of kids for the first time, I mentioned that you can more quickly gain acceptance by the group if you're willing to initially play smaller team roles.

Consider applying this same approach to your overall game.

When you're playing with better players (which may be much of the time), you will need to concentrate on the specific roles you can play well. You will need to maximize your strengths, and avoid your weaknesses.

Almost everyone has different strengths and weaknesses. Even if you're less athletic than many of your friends, it's likely that you possess some ability that you can use to your advantage—a way to compensate.

For example, you may be at a stage in your development where you lack good hand-eye coordination. Consequently, you struggle throwing and catching a ball. But you may be strong—able to box-out and rebound the ball well in a game of basketball, or block others in a pickup football game. You may be smart and understand patterns of movement, and consequently have a knack for anticipating what will happen next. If you're quick, but small, you may be able to play excellent defense.

Try to focus on your positive attributes and understand how you can apply them to your game. If you do, you will contribute to your team and your friends will want you to be part of their games.

Stand Up for Yourself

When playing pickup, you will face a few players who view playing sports from a very simple perspective: Winners win—Losers lose. To these players, winning is everything. Their self-esteem is directly tied to achieving that goal. These players will use gamesmanship, mental warfare, and other questionable tactics to try and secure victory. They may bend the rules or make "bad calls" to gain advantage.

For instance, in a game of pickup basketball, you might cleanly block your opponent's shot. But he or she counters your good defensive play by saying that you committed a foul. Likewise, when you steal the ball, this type of player will call "foul"—even though there was little or no body contact. You can also expect this opponent to claim that "they never touched the ball" in a situation where they slightly deflect the ball out-of-bounds.

Though everyone makes the occasional bad call (and sometimes gets caught defending it), you need to watch for the opponent who regularly does so. Against these players you need to decide how to handle their behavior.

If you're a beginner or new to a group, you may want to take it slow at first. Your opponent may have special standing within the group and you may be viewed as an outsider. In these situations, consider questioning the call once. Do so without emotion. Force your opponent to make a statement defending his or her call. This puts your opponent on notice that you will not passively accept every bad call.

Even when you're familiar with other players, you may decide it's simply not worth the emotional effort to argue a call. You may not want to push the issue beyond a couple of comments.

But understand that there's a risk to not challenging others who repeatedly manipulate the situation to their advantage. You lose respect.

Your teammates expect you to stand up for yourself and your calls. They expect you to speak up when *you're* fouled. When you don't, you give your opponent and his or her team an advantage. Since your teammates want to win, you will lose their respect should you continually back down.

You also lose respect from your opponent. Against players who often make self-serving bad calls, you must forcefully meet them head-on. Otherwise, you'll keep getting run over. Much like confronting a bully, you need to stand your ground. It's not fun arguing. It ruins the flow of the game. But once your opponent realizes you're not going to easily give in, his or her behavior often changes (at least for that game). Your battle with your opponent returns to one of pure competition.

The Player Nobody Wants

In pickup games everyone likes to get chosen early, preferably first or second. But within any group of players, there will always be less skilled players who are the last ones chosen. Sometimes even a talented player (the selfish one that hogs the ball, takes far too many shots, and makes the game less enjoyable for his teammates) is a lower pick.

It takes a special type of player, however, to get branded as the *worst* player—the one that elicits a collective groan from everyone each time that person shows up to play. But before you jump to any conclusions, it's not necessarily the least-skilled player.

To help illustrate the fatal flaw that leads to a player's downfall, let's have some fun with a fictional character named Joe. We'll pretend that he *is* the worst player and look at how his behavior affects the other players' view of him. You can plug in the sport of your choice.

Our imaginary scenario begins with Joe arriving to play in a pickup game. He's played with this group before and they know who he is. A few players greet him, but most just ignore him. Teams are picked and he's the last player chosen. He can't understand why. In his mind, his abilities are equal to, or exceed, those of some other players. The game begins. Part of him realizes that some of his teammates are better, but he also feels that he has the "right" to touch the ball as much as anyone else. Why should they have all the fun? So when his team is on offense, and the ball comes his way, he proceeds to "do his thing." He may be aware (but probably not) that his teammates are grumbling about his play. The game ends. His team loses. He tried hard and gave it his best effort. He can't understand why his teammates are ignoring him.

Most likely, you can see what Joe can't. That his view of playing sports revolves around himself instead of his team. That he believes he is entitled to do what everyone else on the team does, regardless of whether he has the ability to succeed. That he doesn't understand the important concept of playing a role in team sports. And finally, that his play directly affects the fortune of other players on the team.

The key to acceptance

It's essential for you to understand that a single player in most team sports has the power to disrupt a team's effectiveness and opportunity to win. Since most players like to win (especially when a win means "staying on" for the next game), they will avoid any such individual.

The key to acceptance by others in a team game is to have an accurate understanding of both one's ability and the corresponding team role(s) that best match your skills and talent. Grasp these two points, realistically shape your game to accentuate strengths and diminish weaknesses, and you will always have value to other players. Even if your ability is limited, your teammates know that *you* understand your limitations, will "play within yourself," and can look past your personal needs to help the team maximize its opportunity to win. If you demonstrate this quality, other players will respect you.

Players who think they are better than they actually are—and refuse to play a role that fits their abilities—will continually fail. They will fail to make necessary plays while also committing errors that pull their team down. If you engage in this behavior, consciously or not, other players will avoid playing with you. Should you continue to demonstrate this fatal flaw of judgment or character, others will unfortunately brand you as—the *worst* player.

▶ If you sense other players avoiding you, choosing you last in pickup games, or not passing to you when you're open, it's time to realistically examine your game. Are you hogging the ball, taking too many shots, or attempting plays that are beyond your skill level? How many errors and turnovers occur when the ball is in your hands? Ask your friends for their thoughts and advice. Although it may be hard for you to do, try to see beyond your ego.

While the above example describes a pickup game, the same principle applies to organized sports. Although your teammates may not control your playing time, they will resent your style of play, ignore you, or may even make fun of you. The team's coach will either minimize your playing time or (in the case of competitive programs) cut you from the team.

If your ability and skills are, or become, superior to other players, your team role will inevitably and naturally grow. Don't try to force this process; don't try to be something you're not. Know yourself, know your team, and know your role.

When in doubt, stick to the basics and help your teammates succeed. In basketball, for example, you might concentrate on making good passes, playing solid defense, and setting screens to free other players. By taking this approach, you will quickly find acceptance (and gain confidence).

Beware of Brothers Who Argue

The prior scenario illustrated how a single player's ego can spoil a team's opportunity to win. While some players hurt their team, others ruin the pickup game itself. These are the individuals whose attitude and approach to playing is so disruptive that the integrity and flow of the game are affected.

These individuals also elicit a collective groan from other players when they show up to play. They are viewed much the same as the "worst player" described above.

Although anyone can potentially spoil your game, be especially wary of brothers (and sisters) who incessantly argue.

Rarely is a large neighborhood pickup game played that doesn't include a brother or sister combination; many of your games wouldn't be the same without them. But some boys and girls will concede nothing to their sibling. At their worst, these kids will wreck your neighborhood pickup game. Their arguments will continually stop the play. The players who enjoy the play itself will become frustrated and lose interest. The game's momentum will falter and players will start to leave. Game over.

⬤⁎If you're playing with your brother or sister, try to suppress your sibling rivalry; otherwise, you may find that your arguments result in other players excluding you from the neighborhood games. (Also beware of competitive relationships with your friends.)

When I was in high school, a family with two brothers moved onto our street. We invited them to play touch football with us, but found that they continually argued about everything—the spot of the ball, whether they were touched by a defender when they ran with the ball, and who was responsible for a good or bad play. Nothing went unchallenged and the flow of the game was ruined. We soon discovered that having both of these guys in the same game was intolerable and avoided it at every opportunity.

PART II:

Becoming a Better Player

Principles of Play

I want to take my game to the next level.
Can you tell me more about game strategies
and tactics?

... Mike

Playing sports involves more than athleticism and well-executed sports skills. There is also the mental side of the game—the behaviors, strategies, and tactics that help support quality play. In various combinations, these elements form principles of play—rules of conduct and patterns within the play that lead to success.

No matter your level of athleticism, it's essential that you understand your sport's principles of play. This knowledge can help you play more effectively now; it's also a gateway to success at higher levels of play. It can provide you with a competitive advantage.

While some of these principles only pertain to a single sport, others are readily applied across *many* sports. For instance, a good grasp of player movement patterns, spacing, and "angles" can create opportunities to gain advantage in sports such as soccer, basketball, hockey, lacrosse, and tennis.

This chapter covers principles of play that are common to most sports. Let's begin by taking a look at some basic behaviors and tactics that can improve your individual play. We'll then examine some of the principles that relate to team play.

Change it Up (Speed, Style of Play)

Once you've conquered the basics of a sport, you will benefit from mixing up your style of play, changing speeds, and otherwise employing variations of technique that confuse your opponent.

Consider a baseball pitcher who possesses an outstanding fastball. At lower levels, this pitcher can dominate opposing batters. But at higher levels, the hitters are better. They have quicker bat speed. They identify and process visual clues more rapidly and know how to begin their swing earlier. A pitcher who can only pitch one way—in this case using a fastball—will find less success. Now consider another pitcher who not only throws a good fastball, but also complements this pitch with a curveball or change-up. Batters who face this other pitcher don't know what to expect. They can't "sit" on the fastball. And with confusion and hesitation, the pitcher gains an advantage.

This principle applies in many other situations. Although you may not have exceptional foot speed, *changing* speeds will often enable you to gain separation from your opponent. Your opponent may not react well to your changes in speed. The best receivers in football use this ability to their advantage. They don't always run their routes at full speed. Instead, they may slow down at a point in the route, and then apply a burst of speed to fool their opponent. Players in virtually every team sport can change speeds to deceive their opponent and gain separation.

💣 Although you may *now* have an athletic ability or sports skill that enables you to dominate your opponents, this may not be sufficient to succeed at higher levels of play.

There are still other ways to mix it up. A baseball pitcher can not only change a pitch's speed and style (e.g., fastball vs. curveball), but also change its *location*. First pitching high and inside, and then low and outside, is a sequence of pitches that is more likely to catch the batter off-guard then two pitches to the same location.

Think of your own sport and how you can mix things up. There are opportunities to do so in every sport. Here are a few more examples:

- Much like a baseball pitcher, a tennis player wants to regularly change the type of serve (flat, kick, slice), its location, and speed. During a rally, an accomplished tennis player will sometimes change the rhythm of the rally by hitting a slice shot instead of one with topspin—possibly resulting in a return dumped into the net by an opponent who mishandles the sudden change in spin.

- If you're defending a basketball player located on the low post who is "backing you down," meet those pushes with equal push-back—but then let up briefly so your opponent loses a little balance. Constantly change your defensive position to make it harder for your opponent to adapt. First play behind your opponent, then quickly move to the side and in front, possibly confusing the guard trying to make an entry pass.

Finally, there are some players who *do best by maximizing their dominant, exceptional quality*. Their formula for success is to maximize their strengths. Adding other techniques, ones that are poorly executed, only seems to diminish their success. Although talented in one area, they are not so in others.

But for most players (either those with average abilities or ones who want to play at the highest levels) the ability to change styles, speed, and tactics will add value to their game. In the long run, you will likely find greater success by having more than one golf club in your bag.

The Eyes Have It

It's standard advice to anyone throwing or shooting a ball to "keep your eyes on the target." Same goes for making a pass. But in sports where you're defended, you often need to hide your intention. You need to make your opponent think one thing, while you do another.

Good defenders anticipate what action their offensive counterpart is about to take. They do this by understanding the situation, options available, and the most likely choice. But they also anticipate by observing their opponent's behavior. One of the main behavioral clues is where the offensive player is looking.

Lesser players tend to stare at their target. When passing a ball, for example, they look at their teammate well before they make the pass. Their intention is obvious. As players from past generations would say, "They *telegraph* their pass."

So how do you make an accurate pass or throw without directly looking at your teammate?

You usually *do* look at your target—but only for a split second immediately before the pass or throw. By using your peripheral vision (or taking a quick glance to the opposite side), you know where your teammates are located. You set up the scene in your mind's eye. If your teammates are moving, you then anticipate where they will be when you make the pass or throw. This is the process an experienced player uses when he or she makes a "no-look" pass. (But again, in most instances, you should look at your target just before you act.)

As you become a better player, use your eyes to deceive your opponents. "Look off" a defender prior to making a pass. Look first toward a teammate other than the one to whom you will make the pass. Similar to a physical fake (i.e. faking the actual pass), this deception is effective against defenders who depend on observation and anticipation.

▶ The best NFL quarterbacks like Peyton Manning and Tom Brady are masters of "looking off" safeties on long passes.

Play the Ball
(Don't Let it Play You)

If you've played baseball, you likely learned that to best field a ground ball, you need to move forward toward the ball as it's approaching you. By doing so you control the point at which the ball reaches your glove, making it easier to field. Should you stand still and wait for the ball to reach you, the ball may take a hard-to-handle short hop. (In baseball parlance, "The ball will eat you up.")

This principle, in a more general way, applies to other situations in sports. By being proactively aggressive, you take control of situations as opposed to them controlling you. You dictate the conditions (even in defensive circumstances). You provide yourself with more opportunities to succeed. You further bolster your confidence, while possibly lessening your opponent's.

For instance, if you're defending an outstanding player in a team sport, you have two choices: (1) defend your opponent *after* he or she receives the ball, or (2) defend your opponent *before* the ball is received. The first approach requires you to react to your opponent's actions. At this point, you may be helpless to handle your opponent's considerable offensive skills (or you may need to foul your opponent to prevent a score). The second approach, on the other hand, is one in which you dictate the conditions. You aggressively try to *deny the ball* from ever reaching your opponent. You choose to defend another part of your opponent's game—the ability to get open and receive a pass. Without the ball, he or she can't score. You negate an entire part of your opponent's game. And just as important, your aggressive defense may psychologically "take your opponent out of the game." Without the ball, your opponent may be the one who becomes passive and ineffective.

Similarly, you can deny your opponent the opportunity to dictate play in individual sports. For example, a tennis player may choose to regularly serve and volley against a baseline player who doesn't possess a good return (or who wants long rallies).

To the opposite, if you're passive, you will likely lose control of the play and subject yourself to more of those "short hops" that lead to errors. But it's not just that. You will also miss out on opportunities to make big plays—the home runs that sometimes win a contest.

In describing his frustration over his team's lack of a punt return game, the NFL coach, Wade Phillips wryly said of his punt returner, "He's not really a punt returner, he's more of a punt catcher." Like most NFL coaches, Wade was looking for his punt returner to make plays. Simply catching the ball (or watching it bounce and roll dead) wasn't good enough. Wade knew his team's chances of winning were improved by the occasional big play.

And it's not just missing out on the big plays. Passively *watching and reacting* almost always leads to mediocre performance. You are back on your heels and off balance, not only in a physical sense, but also in a psychological one. You're on the defensive and this tends to sap your confidence over time.

Instead of watching, you need to proactively engage—and do so at a point where you can more easily control the play and outcome. For instance, if you're a basketball or hockey player helping out a beaten teammate in a defensive situation, you shouldn't wait until the attacking player is close to the goal and about to score. Instead, if possible, engage the opponent earlier to prevent a score (and avoid fouling the player as he or she shoots).

Of course there are situations and match-ups where you need to be defensive and selectively look for opportunities to attack. But these are ideally under your control. You choose to play more conservatively. You set up your opponent for your counterpunch. You're the spider, weaving the web.

Don't Just React—Anticipate

In most sports, the ability to react quickly in a controlled way is a valuable physical trait. Speed and quickness often trump other physical characteristics such as size and strength. As many coaches are fond of saying, "Speed kills."

Getting somewhere or to something before your opponent—either through speed, quickness, or a combination of both—

provides you with a competitive advantage. With quick reaction time, you can better defend your opponent, get to a ball or location before others, separate yourself from an opponent, and make instinctive physical movements that benefit your play.

But there is another way to get somewhere before others do— one that lies in your head, rather than your body.

Instead of relying strictly on your physical skills to respond, you can *anticipate* an event and begin moving earlier, in the best way, and ahead of an opponent's action. You can process information more quickly and accurately. Where others miss important clues, you can visualize a ball's current and future trajectory, read an opponent's body position and "game," and recognize time/space relationships of player and ball movements—all of which signal you that a specific event is about to happen. And with this information, you can begin reacting *before* the event occurs.

Here are some examples of the role anticipation plays in different sports when played at their highest level:

- Basketball players (when rebounding a ball) know exactly where a missed shot is going, even before the ball hits the rim.

- Baseball outfielders react immediately after the ball is hit— selecting the direction and rate of speed needed to get to where they expect the ball will eventually land.

- Tennis players returning a serve evaluate the server's motion before the ball is hit to determine both the type of serve and targeted location. This information enables players to more quickly reposition themselves, providing more time to play the ball.

- Hockey players skate to where the puck is going to be—not where it is.

- Soccer goaltenders instantaneously process key information as players attack the goal—evaluating their movements, relationship to each other, and any other clues that suggest which player will take the shot and what area of the goal they will target. Hope Solo's diving save against Japan in the 2012 Olympics gold medal match is one example. Protecting the near post, she anticipated the Japanese player's shot to the far side.

How does one obtain this skill? A few players seemingly have a knack for instinctively anticipating patterns of play. One of the better rebounders in the history of the NBA, Dennis Rodman, was shorter than many of his opponents. Yet he led the NBA in rebounding for seven straight years, in no small part due to his ability to know where a missed shot would go before others did. For players like Rodman, their uncanny ability is possibly a gift, similar to another player's natural athleticism. But anyone can improve their ability to recognize patterns of play and anticipate events. It's a learnable skill.

Like your physical sports skills, this ability is best realized when it becomes a subconscious process. You need to reach the point where you "feel" the patterns of play. You "know" something is about to happen before it does. Your eye and mind pick up subtle clues, recognize patterns, process the possible alternatives, and generate an almost instantaneous response—without using the conscious part of your mind.

💣*Although anticipation can improve your reaction time, beware failing to act because you anticipate an event that *doesn't* happen (e.g., an official's call, the ball going out). Always play hard "to the whistle" and act when in doubt!

As mentioned above, the good news is that your ability to reflexively interpret patterns of play (instead of experiencing a blur of disconnected detail) is learnable. The bad news is that there appear to be few shortcuts to obtaining this ability. You only develop this information processing ability through many hours of play and practice. Analysis and observation can help you recognize possible event triggers ("keys"), but experience is the driving factor in developing the needed real-time recognition and reflexive response.

So if you want to improve your virtual

reaction time through anticipation, you need to experience more repetitions. Although you may benefit from specialized drills or simulations, the easiest way to increase repetitions is to simply spend more time playing and practicing your sport (or other sports with similar patterns of play).

Advantage/Disadvantage

Most patterns of play in sports involve two opponents (individual or team) that initially have no advantage. But inevitably, of course, one side gains an advantage and the other is placed at a disadvantage. Sometimes this results from individual match-ups in which one player or team begins to physically dominate the other. At other times, an advantage is gained by executing certain tactics (offensive play, defensive scheme, etc.).

Throughout this book we touch on ways in which you can both take advantage of and counter physical mismatches. Let's now look at advantage/disadvantage situations from the perspective of tactics.

Besides understanding the general patterns of play that will gain you or your team an advantage, you also need to learn the tactics to use when you are at a disadvantage. You need to know both how to defend your weakened tactical position and, ideally, how to regain a position of either neutrality or advantage.

Positional tactics

During the course of play, teams and players are constantly jockeying positions, each trying to gain the high ground—the position in which they have the best chance to dominate the opposition. A "big man" in basketball tries to post-up his defender on the block. A tennis doubles team wants to be at the net. Hockey and soccer teams try to play in their opponents "end." A defensive end in football, tries to get the "edge" when speed rushing. And of course, each opponent in the above examples is trying to prevent the other side from gaining a dominant position.

Consider a baseline rally between two tennis players (see diagram). At the outset, each player is located in the middle of the court. Neither has an advantage over the other. But as the rally continues, one player (X2) starts to control the play, hitting return shots at sharper angles, moving the other player (X1) farther to one side of the court. Through the use of a well-executed sequence of shots, advantage has swung toward X2.

Tennis: Advantage/Disadvantage

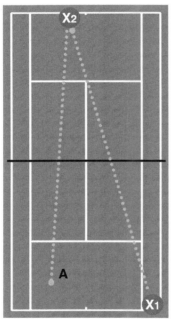

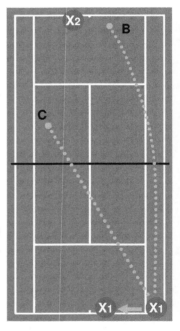

If pulled off the court, player X1 is at a disadvantage. What are X1's options?

A: Returning the ball to player X2 using a normal groundstroke will likely result in a lost point.

B: Hitting a softer, elevated shot will provide an opportunity for player X1 to move back toward the center of the court and keep the point alive.

C: A more difficult and risky option is to hit either a low, sliced shot or hard topspin one into the opposite server box. This can sometimes give the advantage back to player X1 (and even win the point).

On the defensive, and out of position, X1 knows that X2 will eventually try to hit a winner to the opposite side of the court. X1 needs to understand the possible shots (e.g., deep, elevated, slightly cross-court shot with less pace) that can defuse the inevitable winner *before* play gets to that point. And if X2 does attempt to hit a winner, X1 also needs to know how best to return the ball (e.g., defensive lob) should it be reached.

Positional tactics are of course specific to each sport. Just as the tennis players in the above example need to know how to both move their opponent around and recover when out of position, a wrestler needs to understand how to gain position and counter his opponent's moves to do the same. Besides learning the skills associated with your sport(s), you must also learn its positional tactics.

Number mismatches

In team sports such as hockey, basketball, lacrosse, and soccer, there are often two-on-one and three-on-two situations.

What do you do when you're outnumbered? For example, what do you do when you're the defensive "one" on a two-on-one fast break by your opponents toward your goal? Depending on your sport, there are several tactics you can use.

- In *hockey*, where a goalie is defending the net, you ultimately need to defend the pass to the opposite player, leaving your goalie to handle the shot from the player driving toward the goal.

- In *soccer*, you would use the same tactics if the ball was on the outside. But because of the larger goal, you need to defend the player with the ball driving in from the center of the field. (A shooter has a much larger target area when attacking from the inside.)

- In *basketball*, you would drop back toward the basket (playing a one man zone) and possibly feint the player with the ball, induce a poor pass, and maybe intercept it.

Notice that your responsibilities and tactics defending a 2-on-1 depend on your sport and other factors such as whether a goalie is present. But even with their differences, each sport shares similar tactics in certain situations. In the hockey example above, the defender would initially try to slow down the break farther from the goal should the opportunity present itself. Most sports share a similar objective in situations like this—to induce a bad pass or force a few extra passes to enable teammates to get back and eliminate the numbers mismatch.

Two-on-One

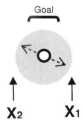

Goal

X₂   X₁

In defending a two-on-one situation, you typically cover a zone area and try to delay and disrupt the offensive attack. The tactics used depend on the sport (i.e., is there a goalie).

There are also specific tactics to employ *when you're on offense*, depending on whether you or your opponent holds the odd-man advantage. Should you enjoy the two-on-one advantage just described, you can aggressively drive toward the defender. This can open up a pass to your teammate should the defender commit to stopping you. In the opposite situation where you're outnumbered (such as when facing a defensive double-team), you can make a well-timed pass to a teammate to neutralize the pressure.

Advantage gained through transition

Offensive advantage is often gained by quick transitions. These can result from either player or ball (puck) movement. Upon a change in possession, a team can often gain an advantage by executing a break toward the opponent's goal. Should the defense not immediately react, the offense will enjoy a 2-on-1, 3-on-2, or similar odd-man advantage.

▶ In team sports with goals, look to the weak (opposite) side for easy scoring opportunities. Players who receive a pass from you will often have an open shot.

In non-breakaway situations (e.g., half-court offense), quick ball movement can result in open scoring opportunities on the weak side. This is most evident against zone defenses. Offensive players can reverse/swing the ball from one side to another through a series of passes or a skip pass. Because the zone cannot transition fast enough to the opposite side, open space exists for a player to receive a pass and possibly score.

Scoring opportunities in individual sports also arise out of quick transitions. As shown in the above tennis example, the winner comes when the ball is finally hit to the open area away from the prior shots.

Stuff Happens Away From the Ball

When you're first learning how to play sports, it's natural for you to focus your attention on the action around the ball (or puck in hockey). Your first instinct is to either move toward the ball to make a play or prepare yourself to receive a pass. It's all about the ball—where it is, how to get it, and what to do when it's in your hands. Even as you gain experience, you may still tend to focus much of your attention on what's happening around the ball.

You should understand, however, that you don't need the ball to help yourself and your team. Opportunities to make plays and gain advantage *without the ball* are available elsewhere on the field of play.

Creating opportunities away from the ball

To recognize these opportunities, you need to direct part of your attention to what's going on *away* from the ball, how it's affecting the game, and what you can do to influence the game without necessarily touching the ball. These opportunities to gain advantage fall into one of two categories:

1. Ones in which you *initiate* actions to set up an opportunity.

2. Ones in which you *react* to an opponent's mistake.

Let's take a look at an example that illustrates both of these types of opportunities. In basketball, you can potentially create a scoring opportunity by setting a screen for the player who you pass the ball to. The player receiving the pass can use your screen and either drive to the hoop for a layup or pull up for an outside shot. (This "on-ball" screen also sets up a possible "pick and roll" or "pick and pop" play.)

But as the diagram below illustrates, you can also move *away* from the ball to set a screen for a teammate on the other side of the court. In this instance you are *initiating* an "off-ball" action that will create a possible scoring opportunity (X3 uses your screen and receives a pass from X2 for a layup).

But sometimes another option presents itself in this situation—one that falls into the second category of *reacting* to an opponent's mistake. It's less obvious, but may be more effective in creating a scoring opportunity.

Imagine you're the left guard (X3) and you see your defender looking away from you toward the point guard (X1) dribbling the ball at the top of the key. If your defender makes this mistake, you can cut "backdoor" toward the basket, receive a pass from your point guard, and score a layup. In this case, your defender has momentarily forgotten about you, and focused too much attention on the ball. (Note that the backdoor play is used not only in basketball, but also in several other sports including soccer, lacrosse, and hockey.)

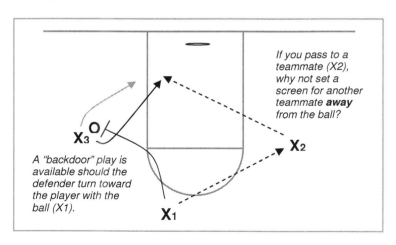

If you pass to a teammate (X2), why not set a screen for another teammate **away** from the ball?

A "backdoor" play is available should the defender turn toward the player with the ball (X1).

Other sports present similar opportunities to gain advantage when a defender's center of attention is solely on the action around the ball. In football, for instance, ball fakes and deception work because some defenders focus too much of their attention on getting to the ball and not enough on the subtle movements and other clues away from the ball that indicate a play's true nature. (The actions of the offensive lineman, for instance, will often tell defenders whether the play is a pass or a run.)

Other opportunities

Let's take a look at a couple of other ways in which you can pro-actively create an off-ball opportunity to gain advantage. Against man-to-man defenses, you can sometimes do so by simply moving to a different spot. This will vacate the space you previously occupied and enable a teammate to move into, and take advantage of, the same space. For example, a teammate with the ball can drive into an area you just "cleared out," one that is closer to the goal and provides a better chance to score.

Clearing Out Space

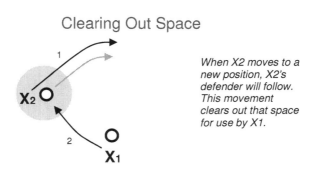

When X2 moves to a new position, X2's defender will follow. This movement clears out that space for use by X1.

Still another possibility to create advantage in the above situation is for the X2 to take his or her defender away from a spot and then quickly return to it. This is especially effective when an offensive player wants to receive a pass in a specific spot, but is aggressively defended in a way that denies the pass or the desired position. A basketball forward who wants to set up on the "block" near the basket may first need to take his defender away from that spot. The forward then returns to the block, ideally with the defender trailing behind. Likewise, a guard who wants to receive a pass within his or her shooting range might first need to drive his player toward the basket and then V-cut back to the desired spot on the court.

Gaining the Position *You* Want

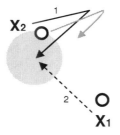

X2 takes his or her defender away from the desired position, and then quickly returns to it. X2 is now open to receive a pass from X1.

There are *many* things you can do without having the ball in your hands. To improve your play, try to raise your awareness of the entire "world" around you. Always be aware of the plays you can make away from the ball and try to recognize all aspects of game situations. When you're on defense, of course, the same principles apply. But in this case, you want to recognize your opponent's tactics and deny the advantage he or she is seeking away from the ball.

Why You Should Play Chess

To play a sport well, you need to understand how player and ball movements affect the game. You must consider not only a single move, but also a sequence of movements. Ideally, you can visualize the effect of alternate movement sequences before they happen.

To begin training your mind to think more tactically, you may want to learn how to play the board game of chess. Playing a good game of chess requires that you analyze the positions of pieces on the board (both yours and your opponent), understand their roles, and visualize how a movement, or succession of movements, will affect your advantage. Good chess players can easily see 3 to 4 moves ahead, both for themselves and their opponents.

This analytical process (also useful to coaches and managers) is similar to the one you use at certain moments while playing sports. Of course, chess is a slower paced game. Events occur quickly in sports, without much time for players to react. But the principle is the same—recognizing player positions and movement patterns, responding with the appropriate action, and ideally doing so ahead of your opponent. Because of the speed with which athletic events unfold, the best players have the cognitive ability to see multiple possibilities and consequences before they occur. As discussed in the topic "Don't Just React—Anticipate" (pg. 88), this real-time anticipative ability during a game is largely a subconscious process developed through experience.

Let's take a look at an example (see diagram) that illustrates the various possible opportunities that can exist in a game situation. We'll examine these opportunities from the perspective of each of three basketball players (you're the guard on the far left of the court).

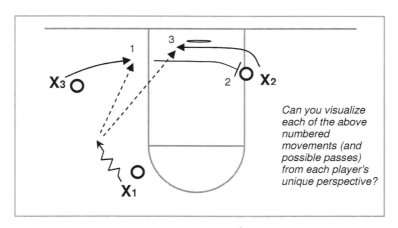

Can you visualize each of the above numbered movements (and possible passes) from each player's unique perspective?

As the wing guard (X3), you may see your opponent briefly looking away from you toward the point guard (X1) with the ball at the top of the key. You also see open space between you and the basket, and instantly recognize the opportunity for you to cut "backdoor" and possibly receive a pass for a layup. But that's not all. At the same time, you may also see one of your teammates (X2) positioned on the low post on the opposite side of the key. You

The Young Athlete's Guide to Playing Sports

immediately recognize the secondary opportunity to set a screen (after your cut) on the opponent defending your teammate—enabling your teammate to quickly move across the lane and possibly receive the ball for a layup.

The point guard with the ball, understanding your style of play, and also seeing the same opportunities, anticipates your actions and looks for the backdoor and low post screen events to unfold while also considering other alternatives. Likewise, the low post player is aware of your possible actions, and is ready to take advantage of the screen, should it occur. As you can see, there is a complex web of possible movements and actions that can potentially lead to your team scoring a basket—if you and your teammates recognize them.

The opportunity to use this cognitive skill is present in all team and individual sports. For example, the best tennis players not only possess outstanding physical and racquet skills but also understand court tactics—how to sequence their shots to move an opponent into a position that opens the court for a final winning shot.

To improve your game, develop your mind's ability to visualize and process sequences of multiple movements. Ideally, you always want to be two moves ahead of your opponent. Play a little chess to help jumpstart your mind's ability to recognize and evaluate potential opportunities that appear during a contest.

💣*Chess requires patience to both learn and play! (Computer chess games have single player, beginner modes that enable you to learn and play chess by yourself.)

Games within the Game

When you first begin playing a team sport such as soccer, basketball, hockey, or lacrosse, you will likely be confused by the movement patterns on offense. It may seem to you that the ball and your teammates are moving in a helter-skelter fashion, with no discernible pattern to their movements. This is especially true when you're playing pickup games or you're on a team that uses a "free-lance" offense (one with no set plays).

You need to understand that seemingly complex patterns of play in a game are often a series of smaller movement sequences strung together. Each of these smaller components is usually a "two-man" or "three-man" game. These *mini-games* involve two or three players on offense running simple plays against the same number of defenders.

As you become more experienced, you will naturally recognize opportunities (player location and spacing) to initiate these mini-games. And if you understand the movement options and patterns of play associated with the mini-game, you will know what do— even within the flow of a much more complex play pattern.

How do you learn the various play patterns that support these mini-games? Besides instruction from a coach, these play patterns are best learned by playing actual two-on-two and three-on-three small-sided games—either in a pickup setting or in the course of an organized sport practice. Pickup games are especially beneficial; they provide the needed repetitions of play patterns that will develop your ability to quickly recognize opportunities as they present themselves. And as the stimulus/response conditioning becomes ingrained, you will find yourself part of a seamless flow of movements and patterns, playing your sport at a higher level.

Two-man patterns

Two-man patterns are the building blocks of most offensive schemes and individual plays. Though there are many two-man patterns and variations, there are several fundamental ones that you must know.

One of the most basic and widely used two-man patterns is the *Give and Go* play; it's used in every team sport. In this play, you pass the ball to a teammate (the "give"), and then cut toward a different location (the "go") to receive a return pass. This simple play can be executed anywhere within the field of play. It's also an effective scoring play close to an opponent's goal—especially against defenders who tend to watch the ball.

101

Give and Go

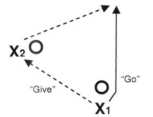

The "Give and Go" is one of the most basic two-man plays in team sports. It's useful in different situations (e.g., scoring, escaping defensive pressure).

Consider a similar formation of players. Can you see another possible play? What if X2's defender looks away toward the player with the ball (X1)? If that occurs, X2 can cut behind the defender and receive a quick pass (and possibly score if close to the goal). As mentioned in the prior two topics, this is referred to as a *Backdoor* play.

Backdoor

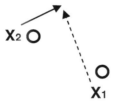

The "Backdoor" two-man play is effective against defenders who aggressively deny passes or ones who tend to focus on the ball.

Setting a screen for a player with the ball, and then rolling (or slipping) toward the goal for a pass is another example of a simple two-man play. This is called a *Pick and Roll.*

Pick and Roll

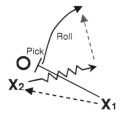

The "Pick and Roll" is another basic two-man play used in some team sports (e.g., basketball, lacrosse).

Similar to the Pick and Roll is the *Pick and Pop*. Instead of rolling toward the goal, the screener steps out away from the goal to possibly receive a return pass from the player who used the screen.

Pick and Pop

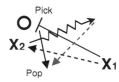

In the "Pick and Pop" the screener pops out to possibly receive a return pass.

Another basic two-man play is the *Outside Handoff*. As two players approach each other, the one without the ball (or puck) crosses behind the player who has the ball. The ball is then passed or handed-off to the crossing player. A variation of this pattern is when the player with the ball is stationary and the other player crosses behind to receive the ball. This play pattern is used in 3-man weaves and many offensive schemes.

Outside Handoff (Cross)

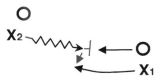

The "Outside Handoff" involves one player crossing behind another to receive a handoff (or pass). Notice that X2 automatically screens X1's defender as the handoff is made.

Still another two-man play, similar to the Give and Go, is the *Kick-Out*. It's especially effective close to the goal. A player located away from the goal (but close enough to shoot), dumps a pass in to a player near the goal. Upon receiving the pass, the player either tries to score or immediately "kicks the ball" (passes) back out to the first player, who then takes an outside shot.

Kick-Out

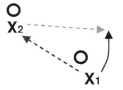

A "Kick-Out" two man play is especially useful against a zone or sagging man-to-man defense

Three-man patterns

Three-man games also have their own set of basic plays. One example is the "screen away" play already discussed in the topic, "Stuff Happens Away from the Ball" (pg. 96). In that play, the player who receives the ball makes a pass to a player who comes off a screen and then cuts toward the goal.

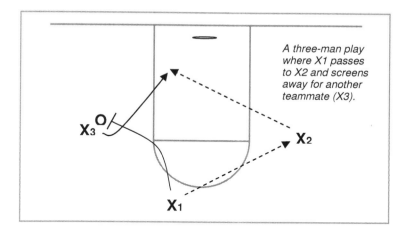

A three-man play where X1 passes to X2 and screens away for another teammate (X3).

Some three-man plays *extend two-man plays*. For instance, if a ball is dumped in from an outside player (X1) to one close to the goal (X2), that player can either try to score, kick it back out to the player who made the pass, *or* pass to a third player (X3) diving toward the goal from the weak-side.

Extending a Two-Man Play Pattern

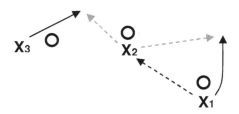

Three-man plays are sometimes an extension of a two-man play. Here, a third player on the weak-side is an additional passing option for the player in the middle.

There are also more complex three-man games that are played within the flow of an offense. One example would be the Triangle offense favored by Phil Jackson, former coach of the Los Angeles Lakers and Chicago Bulls NBA basketball teams. This offense involves a primary pattern that uses three players—a forward in the low post, a guard on the wing, and another player in the corner.

Although the locations of the players and ball are constantly changing, the "triangle" regularly appears, triggering the players to execute specific options.

"Man" and "Zone" Principles

In team sports, players' actions and responsibilities on defense are driven by the type of scheme their team employs. These schemes employ man-to-man principles, zone principles, or a combination of the two.

Man-to-Man defense

In a *man-to-man defense*, each defender matches up against an offensive player, defending the goal from any actions the offensive player may take. The defender follows the assigned offensive player wherever he or she goes, most often taking a position between the offensive player and the goal.

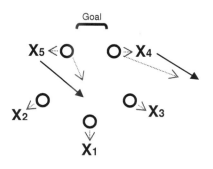

Man-to-Man Defense

Each defender guards a specific offensive player—wherever he or she goes.

Zone defense

Unlike a man-to-man defense, a *zone defense* requires that each defender guard an area on the court or field. Defenders are responsible for any player that comes into their assigned area.

Zone Defense

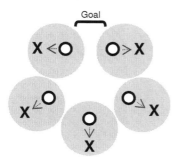

*Each defender is assigned **an area** to defend, guarding whichever player enters the assigned zone.*

Strengths and weaknesses

Each defensive approach has it strengths. A man-to-man defense assigns clear responsibilities to each player (i.e., you need to focus on stopping that one player). A zone defense, on the other hand, provides multiple layers of protection. Both interior and exterior areas of space are defended. If an offensive player beats a defender in one area, there's ideally another defender waiting in the adjacent area.

Likewise, each approach has its own set of weaknesses. A man-to-man defense is more susceptible to a single offensive player wreaking havoc—especially when that team has outstanding scorers. Offenses can more easily use "screens" to free up a player for a scoring opportunity.

A zone defense has "gaps" that an offense can attack; it sometimes cannot react quickly enough to ball movement (passes); and the lack of individual assignment responsibilities can sometimes lead to confusion, missed coverage, and scoring opportunities for the offense.

Because each approach has both strengths and weaknesses, coaches have devised defensive systems that try to combine elements of both.

Combination defenses

There are many variations of these two primary defenses—ones that either borrow from the other to defend specific situations or more explicitly combine both principles into a unique defensive system.

For example, man-to-man defensive schemes always include a secondary help system (see diagram). When a defender is beaten, another defender rotates over to defend the offensive player. If this occurs close to the goal, a defender from the opposite (weak) side will move to defend the offensive player about to score. Weak-side defenders in this situation forego their man-to-man responsibilities to defend a crucial zone. Although this "weak-side help" begins to blur the individual, man-on-man responsibilities, it's essential to the team's overall defensive effectiveness.

Weak-side Help in a Man-to-Man Defense

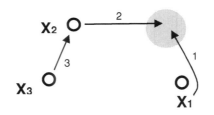

When X1 beats his or her defender to the goal, X2's defender "rotates" over to stop an easy score. X3's defender then rotates down to cover X2.

As mentioned above, there are complex defenses that combine both man and zone principles to varying degree. A "match-up" zone employs man-to-man principles, but players give up their man to another teammate when the offensive player cuts through the zone. In basketball, "combination" defenses (e.g. Box-and-One, Triangle-and-Two) use man-to-man coverage on one or two opponents while the remaining defenders are responsible for defending certain areas. These defenses are typically used when an opponent has one or two exceptional guards who can easily score when defended by a single player. Other sports such as hockey also employ combination defenses (Box Plus One).

Triangle and Two Combination Defense

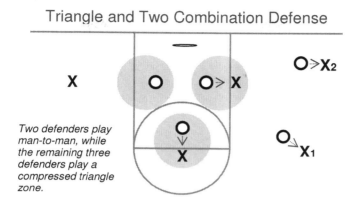

Two defenders play man-to-man, while the remaining three defenders play a compressed triangle zone.

Every team sport has its own set of defensive schemes, but invariably they use some combination of man-to-man and zone principles.

Man and Zone principles also used in offenses

Also keep in mind that these principles can sometimes apply to offensive systems. For example, in football, offensive linemen often use different "zone blocking" schemes. For a given play, the linemen may have individual blocking assignments that do *not* include blocking the player directly opposite them. Instead, they follow specific situational rules and block any player that is occupying a certain area.

Competing for Success

*I like competitive sports, but sometimes feel
I don't play my best in close games. How
can I improve my play in these situations?*

... Sarah

When you were very young, you likely participated in developmental youth sports programs run by adults. Since most of these programs universally emphasized equal participation, you didn't need to worry about getting your share of playing time.

But as you've gotten older, your opportunity to play sports has changed. Some of the programs available to you and other kids your age have become more selective.

AAU (Amateur Athletic Union), Club, and many Travel leagues typically cater to better athletes. High school sports pit teams from different schools against each other. All of these programs share the same quality—they are competitive. You are no longer *entitled* to equal playing time; your playing time is instead determined by how well you play. In many instances, your skill determines whether you even "make the team."

Playing organized sports at the higher levels can bring young athletes many benefits including fun, popularity, and in very few cases, valuable college scholarships or professional opportunities.

Because of these desirable benefits, you *inherently* have competition for both spots on a team and the amount of playing time you receive.

This competitive quality only increases as the rewards become greater. Professional athletes, who sometimes receive millions of dollars for their play, intensely compete with each other for roster spots. They also realize that better performance can lead not only to championships, but also more financial reward.

You can picture this progression from youth sports to the most competitive levels as a pyramid. Its base represents the number of kids who play sports in equal participation youth programs. The pyramid's pinnacle represents the number of people who play sports professionally. As one progresses upward, the opportunity to play becomes more limited and the competition greater.

It's obvious that there aren't many who achieve at the highest levels. (But some do—so don't give up your dreams too easily.)

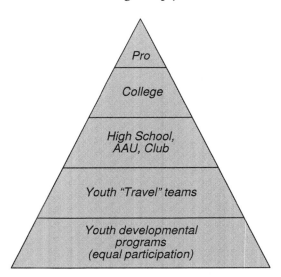

With an understanding of the reality of competitive sports, let's look at how you can improve your ability to compete. In addition to helping you gain more playing time in organized sports, this advice will also help you better compete in pickup games. Remember, players in pickup games are often playing to win so they can stay on the court or field to play more.

It's Okay to Compete

Everyone likes to fit in with other people when they play sports. But do you sometimes give in too easily to your teammates or opponents? Do you quickly back down when confronted or challenged by another player? Are you too nice?

Everyone's personality is different, and you may genuinely be a warm, caring, fun-loving person. This trait will serve you well in casual pickup games and with others who enjoy playing your sport mainly for fun. Getting along with others and resolving conflict by building consensus is important. Your enjoyment of sports will grow through the satisfaction gained from being part of a community that shares similar values.

Understand, however, that *many of your teammates and opponents are different than you* and will take advantage of opportunities that provide them with a competitive edge. They may innately be more competitive, or win-oriented. Their values and reasons for playing the game may vary from yours. Their approach isn't necessarily good or bad, but is different, and you must account for it.

Also, as the competition level increases, you must expect others to have a more competitive attitude. It's not uncommon at higher levels for the best players to play with an "edge." With otherwise pleasant personalities, they give no quarter when competing. They don't back down. The *great* players hate to lose—period.

If you tend to be too nice and always give in to others, seek the middle ground. Assert yourself more often. Stand your ground. Especially in competitive settings, play with a more selfish attitude. By doing so, you will not only maximize your personal rewards but also gain the respect of your teammates and competitors.

In team practices or "friendly" pickup games, try to quickly assess your opponents to determine their personality type and how they're going to play the game. If they're extremely competitive, they may slightly bend the rules or make questionable calls to gain

💣 If your teammates see you unnecessarily conceding to an opponent and not standing up for yourself, you will quickly lose their respect. Your teammates do not want to lose because you're afraid to claim what is rightfully yours.

an advantage. Don't accept this abuse. Instead, match their competitiveness and "name their sins" as they occur. By aggressively challenging these individuals, they will often back down and you will transform your game into one of pure competition.

Sometimes, the most satisfying, intense moments in sport come when you play with an aggressive edge—it brings out the best in both you and your competitor. You can still be nice, but understand that it's all right for you to compete.

Consolidate Your Advantage (It's Yours, Now Hold on Tight!)

Opportunity presents itself in different ways. Sometimes you undergo changes during adolescence that suddenly provide you with a physical advantage. You may also learn how to perform key skills more adeptly, providing you with a competitive edge over other players. Other times an opportunity results from an external event—an injury to a teammate, someone deciding not to go out for the team, or your coach shaking up the lineup (when your team is not performing well).

As a freshman on my high school's basketball team, I seldom received much playing time in games. The team's starters were physically more mature. And unlike many of these boys who could shoot jump shots against defensive pressure, I only possessed a "set" shot. I recall spending many of my freshman year practices on the side of the gym trying to learn how to shoot a jump shot with the ball up over my head.

But by the beginning of my sophomore year's basketball season, I had become stronger—and more importantly—quicker. I also had developed a jump shot and could now score consistently from short range. The team's mix of players had also changed. Two of the prior year's starters decided to focus on football and not go out for the team. From nowhere, I suddenly found myself with an opportunity to compete with the best players on the team. The head coach chose me as one of the team's starters for our opening game and I remained a starter for the rest of the season.

If you're ready for the opportunity, physically or otherwise, *you* can find yourself starting, receiving more playing time, or asked to play a more important role. As this opportunity unfolds, you may also begin to realize that you *can* perform at this higher level.

Once you've tasted success, you need to consolidate (strengthen) your new-found advantage. You do so by stringing together quality performances, one after another. Similar to how repetition locks in an athletic skill, repeatedly performing well in competitions reinforces your sense of the possible and boosts your self-confidence. These successes root within you an unwavering belief that you *will* succeed. This confidence is important for those inevitable moments when you face adversity—when events don't go your way and doubt begins to creep in.

During my sophomore year basketball season, there were many ups and downs. A few of my teammates regularly challenged me in practices, hoping to take my spot as a starter. But once I had tasted success, and realized that I could compete, I stubbornly warded off my teammates' efforts. In one practice after another, I demonstrated that I

● As your role within your team changes and improves, you will likely confront challenges from teammates who don't want to give up their position to you. They may try to intimidate you to see if they can undermine your new found confidence and status. This is natural—not all of your teammates are your best friends and willing to easily accept your good fortune at their expense.

115

was the better player. And with repeated success in doing so, my confidence increased. I fortified my advantage and remained a starter.

Remember that it's a competitive world and everyone wants their piece of it. Recognize your opportunity when it arrives, grab it, and resist the inevitable challenges by others. It's yours, now hold on tight!

Prepare to Compete

Raw talent may be your initial gateway to success. Your body may also develop as you mature, providing you with a competitive advantage.

But as you progress upward on the road to more competitive play, the advantage provided by your innate gifts will lessen. Other factors will come into play.

You'll find that your success will become more dependent on what you do *before* the game begins. Preparation becomes a key ingredient in the formula for success. Conditioning, the learning of new skills, and extensive practice all deepen and strengthen the foundation of your competitive advantage.

The *way* in which you prepare is also important. Spending time lackadaisically practicing your skills is not nearly as effective as doing so in a way that more closely duplicates game conditions. For instance, practicing basketball free throws when you're tired is a better approach than doing so at the beginning of practice. Practicing shots that you normally shoot in a game is a more effective use of your practice time than goofing around shooting from unrealistic distances. Practicing against an opponent teaches you important lessons about how to execute a skill in a way that actually works in a real game. (You may have a beautiful, accurate shot, but one that takes too long to release against defensive pressure.)

When practicing, look for ways to simulate game conditions. Besides playing pickup, shooting games and role-playing can also add value to your practice time. The shooting games you sometimes play with your friends create pressure (miss the shot and you lose, or go back to the start). Pretending your playing the role of your sports hero in a certain game situation may help motivate you to learn, practice, and properly execute a certain skill. And who hasn't simulated the importance of making that last second winning shot as we counted down the last few seconds of our imaginary game? Besides simulating certain game conditions, these approaches also inject some fun into your practices. They complement the more rigorous individual drills you practice on your own.

Associated with the commitment to prepare are fundamental behavior patterns—ones that are just as important as the act of preparation itself. These include self-discipline, perseverance, and a willingness to sacrifice short term benefits for greater long-term ones. Together these contribute to a singular work ethic that enables success in both sports and other areas of your life.

A strong work ethic to prepare can enable you to compete against better athletes. Not only will your superior conditioning and hours of practice maximize your ability, but the tough-mindedness you've developed to prepare will also serve you in the competition itself. While others wilt under pressure, you will stubbornly persevere and simply outlast your opponents to reach the finish line first.

Unlike physical gifts, developing a solid work ethic in preparing to play is largely under your control. This may be more difficult for some than others—but it is an act of the mind and a learnable behavior.

Play Up When Possible

Earlier in this book, I discussed how both Playing Up and Playing Down can help you learn and develop your ability to play sports. Playing Up is *essential* for more advanced players who want to get better. If you're a skilled player, you *must* seek out other players of equal or better ability to further improve your game.

When playing in pickup games with superior players, you will quickly learn which of your skills work and which ones don't. These games are your testing ground. You will also have the opportunity

▶ On your own, or in neighborhood games with less skilled players (Playing Down), you can develop and practice new techniques. But eventually, you will need to take these skills to the playground, gym, or playing field to prove their effectiveness. Do so against equal or better competition.

to observe and learn new skills—the ones that help these other players succeed in more competitive play.

Besides Playing Up to learn and test individual skills, this more competitive setting requires that you also learn how to play different, more secondary roles. It forces you to take a new look at your game, and how it fits in with that of your more skilled teammates. Instead of playing the dominant "scorer" role on offense, your value to the team may now lie in how well you play defense and make passes. Learning these other roles builds breadth and flexibility into your game, enabling you to more easily adapt to what you and your team need to succeed.

Try to work your way into games with older or more talented players. You will often encounter resistance from players who don't want to play with younger or less skilled kids. They are also looking to play up. But, even if your skills are limited, you may be the extra player that the group needs to fill out a team and play the game. Persevere and you will find yourself playing in these games.

Seek out opportunities to compete against better competition—Play Up!

Especially for Girls

If you are a strong, competitive girl who is looking to improve, you should play sports with boys. In team sports such as basketball, participate in pickup games; in individual sports such as tennis, practice against boys.

Not only will you more easily locate good competition, but you will probably find that you need to adapt your game to compensate for boys' greater physical strength and explosiveness (on average). You will need to develop new and different skills, adapt to a faster game, and learn how to play with even *more* intelligence to offset any physical disadvantage. All of which can provide you with a competitive advantage when you play against other girls.

NOTE: The Women's Sports Foundation supports a position that girls and boys should be encouraged to compete with and against each other in sports whenever possible.

If you participate in a non-contact sport (golf, tennis) and have exceptional talent, you may even want to consider playing on a boy's team. There are many instances of girls doing so and achieving success. But also understand that you will need to adjust to a different social setting and possibly confront some related hardships.

In both pickup games and organized sports, you may initially face resistance from a few boys who don't want to play with the opposite sex. You may be teased or outright bullied, much the same as a boy who is somehow different. Don't let this deter you. Depending on your personality, you can either ignore the teasing or calmly look the boy in his eye and "call him out." Since many other boys will respect your talent or otherwise want to play with you, try to form allegiances with them. They will likely support you if the teasing gets out of hand.

Boys are sometimes confused about how they should play competitive sports with girls. If you're intent on improving your game, insist that boys treat you the same way as they would another boy. You may need to challenge some boys to do so. In these situations, talk yourself up. For example, suggest to whomever is covering you that he "can't handle your game." On defense you might say, "You can't get past me."

▶ Remember that boys value competency in team sports— especially as it relates to you knowing how to play a role that can help the team win. With most boys, **your play** will define whether you're accepted in the group.

There Are Different Ways to Get a Win

In sports you can win or lose a game in many different ways. Sometimes seemingly insurmountable advantages evaporate when confronted with a particular combination of *strategy, tactics, and skills.* This reality can provide you with your greatest victories, but also bring you heartbreaking losses.

Whether you're favored to win or are the overwhelming underdog, always keep this principle in mind. Your opponent may look physically superior, either in athleticism or skills, but lack in some other less visible area. He or she may not handle pressure well or may make too many unforced errors. To the opposite, your opponent may appear physically inferior, but still have an understanding of the game and its tactics that far exceeds yours—providing your opponent with an advantage that is not fully evident until the contest is well under way.

I learned this lesson during my junior year in high school when I was competing with another player to earn a singles spot on my high school tennis team. I was clearly the better athlete and had more powerful groundstrokes. But in our match for that spot, my teammate won, playing better angles and varying the pace of the game. His command of *game tactics* was superior to mine and provided him with the edge that eventually led to his victory.

As discussed previously, *conditioning* plays a role in who wins a contest. You can sometimes overcome an opponent who has superior athleticism and talent by enduring a higher level of physical (or mental) exertion for longer periods of time. Your advantage will often appear in the latter stages of a competition when fatigue withers your opponent's skills and will to win.

Gamesmanship can occasionally undermine an opponent's capacity to compete. As it relates to playing your sport, you or your opponent may have a better understanding of human nature and try to use it to gain advantage. Player actions, comments (trash talk), and attitude displays will sometimes affect an opponent's state of mind, disrupting that player's concentration. Players susceptible to

120

these tactics are easily taken out of their games, neutralizing their effectiveness.

The incidence of trash talking varies among different groups of players and typically reflects the group's unique culture of play. As a whole, trash talking diminishes the inherent beauty of playing sports. It represents a means of intimidation outside the play itself, and can indicate an overemphasis on winning (at all costs). Although playful trash talking is occasionally okay among friends, avoid engaging in it during more serious competitions. Let your play define your excellence.

Finally, the *environment* in which a game is played also affects the contest's outcome. Fan support, home field advantage, and playing conditions can all play a role in determining a winner and a loser.

At the close of my high school tennis career, my partner and I played in a local doubles tournament. We reached the finals, playing a team from a Catholic city school. Although we were seeded number one, our two opponents clearly had better strokes and a more refined game. Fortunately for us, it was a windy day. The match began and we played poorly. While the wind carried our miss-hit shots well out of bounds, our opponent's superior ground strokes seemed to cut through the wind and give them winner after winner. At first we were grumbling and moaning over our misfortune, then yelling in frustration, and finally laughing in disbelief at our incompetence. But the wind, our wild shots, and antics began to work to our advantage—our opponent's game slowly began to disintegrate. The stop and start, erratic nature of the match disrupted our opponent's flow and concentration. As they began to make unforced errors, we pulled ourselves together, raised the level of our

▶ Don't let your opponent distract or upset you. Once your opponent realizes that trash talk and other intimidating antics can affect your play, you will receive more of the same abuse. Ignore any trash talk and continue to concentrate on playing within each moment. If you do get mad, translate your anger into positive actions—play harder with more focus. Use insults as motivation.

●ᐞ Never grow too confident in your physical ability or skills—realize that game tactics and other factors may play an important factor in determining a contest's victor.

play, and eventually walked away with the championship trophy. Our opponents were disgusted with themselves, unable to comprehend how they lost a match to seemingly inferior players.

Approach your contest with confidence, but don't overlook the possibility that events may conspire against you. Live in each moment of the game, letting your skills and ability naturally exert their dominance, building your advantage over the course of the contest. Always seek to understand the different ways in which a game can be won or lost.

Find and Exploit Your Opponent's Weaknesses

Your ability to play a sport well always starts with your own game. Ideally, you possess an arsenal of skills that give you an edge over your opponents. Any weaknesses you have are minimal. Your game is both strong and resilient. Like a tree buffeted by high winds, it remains standing no matter the fierceness of the storm.

But in a contest that pits you against a tough opponent, you also need to consider the nature of your opponent's abilities and game. You need to understand his or her strengths and weaknesses. By doing so, you can employ tactics that improve your chance of winning. Before or during a contest, try to find and exploit your opponent's weaknesses. Even the best players have them.

Your opponent's "weak side"

Start by determining whether your opponent has a weak side. Athletes typically have a dominant side and a weak one. For instance, tennis players rarely have equally strong forehand and backhand groundstrokes—one is usually weaker than the other. In many sports, a young athlete's weak side is the same as the athlete's non-dominant hand. Right-handed basketball players will usually dribble better with their right hand. Right-footed soccer players will likely dribble the ball better with their right foot. And in both cases, each will find it easier to move to the right (and better protect the ball). For these players, their weakness lies in using their left side and moving in that direction.

So in the above examples, how would you exploit your opponent's weak side? If the tennis player favors his or her forehand, you would of course hit more balls to the backhand side. For the basketball and soccer players, you would defend them by positioning yourself slightly to their right ("overplaying") and forcing them to use their weak hand/foot and move to their left.

Other weaknesses

Your opponent's weaknesses can lie almost anywhere within his or her game. Like the examples just discussed, they may be obvious. Other defects (like an inability to play well in stressful situations, for instance) may be less obvious. Sometimes these subtle weaknesses won't appear unless you force your opponent past a certain threshold. Up until that point, your opponent's play may be flawless. But exert enough pressure over an extended period, and your opponent's game begins to fall apart. Confidence erodes, self-doubt creeps in, focus is lost, and athletic performance falters.

Here are several other examples of potential weaknesses and ways to exploit them:

- *Your opponent has a specific skill area that is exceptionally weak.* Similar to having a weak side, an athlete may have a skill area that is extremely weak. Some baseball batters can hit a fastball, but struggle with curveballs and change-ups. A basketball guard may play well against a passive zone defense, but regularly commits turnovers when dribbling against a pressure

123

man-to-man defense. An offensive football lineman can pass block against a bull rush, but is unable to handle a speed rush on the edge. Once you identify a skill weakness, go after it! (Throw the curveball, pressure the basketball guard when dribbling, and use a speed rush against the offensive lineman more often than a bull rush.)

- *Although possessing excellent sports skills, your opponent is physically deficient in some way.* A skilled player may lack strength, size, foot speed or quickness. If you are quicker, try to deny your opponent the opportunity to use a skill. Against an exceptional offensive scorer, for instance, try to defend this opponent *before* they receive the ball by denying the pass. In racquet sports like tennis, try to move your slower opponent around the court side to side, forward and back, opening the court for an eventual winner. Take advantage of other physical mismatches. In the football example above, use the bull rush against the offensive lineman who has quick feet and good technique, but lacks size or strength. In basketball, consider posting-up defenders who are much smaller.

- *Your opponent relies too much on his or her physical athleticism.* Some athletes ignore (or are unaware of) good tactics because they typically win contests through physical talent alone. Try to counter any athletic or physical advantage with a compensating game strategy and tactics. A good example is the "Rope a Dope" boxing strategy used by Muhammad Ali to sap George Foreman's punching power over the course of their famous fight.

- *Although athletic, your opponent is either not well-conditioned or possesses less endurance than you.* Similar to the previous item— but in this case an athlete is physically ill-equipped for a longer, tougher contest. Against this type of opponent, you try to survive the beginning onslaught, knowing that over the length of the contest the tide will turn as your endurance prevails.

- *Your opponent loves a certain style of play, but does not easily adapt to other styles.* Some athletes love "pace." If you hit a tennis ball to them hard, they return it harder. Against these opponents, mix up your shots. Hit some balls soft and high, others hard and low. Add some spin. Change locations. If you're a baseball pitcher, for instance, mix in some changeups against a good fastball hitter. Sometimes it's not one style that works, but the constant changing of style that wins the day. (See "Change it Up" on page 84 for more on exploiting this weakness.)

Finally, here's an example that illustrates the last item. When I played tennis as a junior in high school, I had the opportunity to watch the deciding set of an important match in which our second singles player was struggling. Although Jay was an excellent player with smooth strokes, his opponent seemed to have figured out his game. Jay's opponent loved pace and was crushing his return at every opportunity. It appeared Jay had little chance to win.

In utter frustration, Jay changed his tactics—*he began to serve underhand.* He hit the ball upward in a looping arc so that when it came down in the service box, it bounced high. Seeing the opportunity to quickly end the point, Jay's opponent charged forward, wound up, and swung to put the ball away. But in his eagerness to end the point, Jay's opponent began to hit the service returns out of play. He struggled hitting the soft "sitter" at shoulder height.

During rallies, Jay began to mix in lobs with regular ground strokes. I watched in disbelief as Jay's opponent grew more and more frustrated, dumping shots into the net and spraying the ball past the end lines. As the match continued, his opponent completely lost his composure and Jay came back to win the match.

In this instance, Jay's willingness to boldly change his tactics exposed his opponent's inability to handle a certain style of play. Although you probably won't have to resort to such an extreme approach, keep probing your opponent to discover where his or her weaknesses lie.

Winning on Paper Means Nothing

It's not unusual for players and coaches to look at an upcoming match-up with an opponent, compare the various strengths and weaknesses, and conclude who has the advantage "on paper."

Do not, however, make the mistake of believing that a victory is guaranteed. Your mind has a tendency to plan ahead, stringing one reasonable assumption after another until a conclusion is reached. The problem is there are always too many variables in the equation of a sports contest to ensure an outcome. Your physical abilities, skill level, and demonstrated capability to win, may all strongly suggest that you will beat an opponent—but you may also unexpectedly encounter injuries, a bad day, or an opponent playing far better than usual.

History is littered with incredible upsets that were considered impossible based on the "paper" advantage of one team over another. For instance, absolutely no one expected the 1980 USA Olympic hockey team (consisting mainly of college players) to compete with, let alone beat, the powerful USSR professional team.

More recently, Virginia Commonwealth University (VCU), an eleven seed in the 2011 NCAA basketball tournament, upset Kansas—the number one seed. Kansas's outside shooting ability inexplicably disappeared, sending this overwhelming favorite to an improbable defeat. For the Kansas faithful, this was but the most recent in a string of unexpected tournament losses. In 2005, my alma mater, fourteenth seeded Bucknell, shocked the number three seeded Jayhawks.

Should you be in the opposite situation, the underdog who appears outclassed by an opponent, remember this same lesson. You cannot know whether your opponent will play poorly or if you will have one of your best days. Unexpected victories will come your way on occasion.

Don't accept any advantage or disadvantage on paper—bring your best effort and play the game to determine who the winner is on that particular day.

It's Not Over Until It's Over (Don't Get Overconfident)

Too often, athletes become over-confident in their abilities, their apparent advantages over an opponent, or a sizeable lead they have gained in a game or match. Even when everything suggests a victory is in hand, momentum sometimes dramatically shifts. Once it does, less talented athletes and teams can prevail.

In contests where talent and skill are evenly matched, but one contestant has built a large advantage, the lead can still amazingly evaporate. An example of this was the 2004 Boston Red Sox victory over the New York Yankees in the American League baseball championship series. Despite the Red Sox being down three games to zero (best of seven), trailing when they began the ninth inning of game four, and having a long history of losing in the playoffs, they strung together an improbable series of plays to climb back into the series and eventually win it. After beating the Yankees, the Red Sox then went on to win the World Series against the St. Louis Cardinals.

Even when a contest is seemingly under your control, concentrate on the moment and do not think that you have reached the finish line. Although unlikely, anything can still happen. Remind yourself of this and stay focused.

When one hears that an athlete displays a "killer instinct," this simply means that the athlete doesn't let up when an opponent is at a disadvantage—but instead tries to increase the lead, and quickly end the contest. This is perfectly acceptable in competitive environments and is a desirable trait for any athlete who wants to succeed at a higher level. If your competition is friendlier (e.g., neighborhood games, playing against younger, less skilled friends), you may want to back off and let others control more of the play.

Also, do not provide your opponent with any emotional incentive that may spur them to raise their level of play—either in the current contest or a future one. Maintain a steady, workmanlike demeanor and take care of business.

During my junior year of high school, we lost a close basketball game at home to our archrival. With a few seconds left, I tried to steal the ball and ended up lying on the court as the buzzer sounded. The other team's star player, who was also an outstanding track hurdler, decided to run and jump over me as I was just starting to get up. Do you think I remembered his behavior the following year when we again faced that team and player? As one of the officials said to our coach after our home victory, "I've never seen a team play with the intensity yours did tonight." Much of that same intensity carried over to our subsequent victory in their gym.

Never become so overconfident that you demonstrate arrogance toward your opponent. Instead, concentrate on maintaining your high level of play (and consolidating any advantage) all the way through to the contest's end. And should you win, celebrate in a way that is respectful of your opponent.

You're Mad—Now Do Something About It!

It's the rare athlete that doesn't occasionally get angry at himself, his opponent, or his coach. You may be mad at yourself for making a stupid mistake. Your opponent may have said or done something that is disrespectful. Maybe you feel that your coach doesn't recognize your ability and has low expectations about your potential to succeed.

When you *do* get mad, your performance can either fall apart or improve—depending on how you react. You can use emotion or be used by it. Successful athletes manage their emotions to improve their play. They transform negative emotion into a positive action.

Why do some athletes play better when they are angry? It's because these individuals have the ability to *channel the energy* of their emotions. This emotional energy provides these athletes with the extra force or focus they need to take their play to a higher level.

128

When I was growing up, a tennis player named John McEnroe was infamous for his court tantrums, regularly berating the match's umpire and often arguing with and glaring at his opponent. Although many fans considered his behavior obnoxious, it was obvious that this man played with more energy and focus when he was mad. He would sometimes search for *any* opportunity to yell at someone, including himself. Meanwhile, some of his opponents, reacting emotionally to his outbursts, would subsequently fall apart, losing their concentration and focus.

> ▶ Emotion can play a huge role in determining a player's effectiveness. Some players thrive on emotion while others perform better by minimizing it. Try to understand which type of player you are.

Another talented tennis star, Andre Agassi, had this to say about using emotion to drive performance: "I've worked to turn that emotion, that anger, into a positive direction instead of negative. Instead of getting me down, that anger can drive me to another level. I feel like I get a shot of adrenaline. Almost like I go into a full court press in basketball." [4]

So how do *you* best handle upsetting situations? Again, this is based on your nature. If you perform better by minimizing emotion or directing it inward, try using relaxation techniques (breathing, imagery, trigger words) to help you suppress and control the emotion.

Otherwise, when you make a significant mistake and do become angry, take the negative emotion and turn it into a specific positive action. Ideally, two responses should occur within you when you become angry.

First, use the emotion to sharpen your concentration. Instead of losing control of your mental state, become more focused, aware, and fiercely resolute in your determination to succeed. Use the anger to fuel this mental state.

Secondly, where possible, funnel the

> ▶ Coaches recognize and appreciate mature players who both control, and use, their emotions to improve their play.

negative emotion into a positive, energy-related *physical* action. For example, you may be the type of player who is a perfectionist. You do not like making avoidable mistakes. While playing offense, you may become mad when you take a bad shot, make a poor pass, or commit a turnover. Instead of hanging your head in dismay or disgust, try to immediately get back and play more intense defense, letting your emotion drive your physical action to a more aggressive (but still controlled) state.

I recently talked with a young woman who is a talented point guard on her high school basketball team. On this subject she echoed the above point saying, "Whenever I make a bad mistake, I always try to make up for it by playing better defense." She also remembered how she reacted when her coach initially suggested to her that if she worked hard she might win a Division II scholarship: "My reaction was 'I'll show coach. I'm going to get a Division I scholarship.'" In each case, this girl translated her anger into a positive response.

You become angry

Sharpen your focus; become resolute

Transform energy into a positive action

Your play improves!

Everyone Loves an Underdog and So Should You

You will face many situations where you're seemingly over-matched against a superior opponent. Possibly you've heard about how good some player is or (at higher levels) read newspaper articles praising the player's talent. Before your game, you may observe how big, tall, or strong your opponent appears. You may notice how the player seems to smoothly execute skills during warm-ups. The player or team may have all of the clothing and equipment accessories, suggesting that they're well-prepared and know what they're doing.

But once a game begins, you will often find that many of the apparent advantages your opponent holds over you are mere illusion. Although physically impressive and athletic, your opponent may not understand how to play the game. Your opponent may also lack a competitive character that equals yours. For example, the tennis player, owner of multiple racquets (in plastic wrap) and beautiful ground strokes, may also possess a game that falls apart at the first sign of pressure. You will encounter many situations where appearances don't match actual ability. Do not put your opponent in the winner's circle or assume you have some inherent disadvantage based on appearances.

There are times when you *are* the underdog—contests where your fundamental talent and skills are inferior to your opponents. But one of the attractive qualities of sports is that a lesser player can sometimes rise up and beat a more talented opponent. You may play above your typical performance level and your opponent may play below their capability. The way in which your abilities and talent match up against your opponent's may also work to your advantage. As Chris Berman, the popular ESPN sportscaster often says, "That's why they play the game."

What seems impossible is sometimes possible. One of the most amazing examples of an athlete performing above their apparent talent level happened in the 1968 Olympics when a long jumper named Bob Beamon won the gold medal. In a track event where the world record was regularly broken by a couple of inches, Bob Beamon jumped 29 ft. 2 ½ inches, 21 ¾ inches better than the prior world record. Don't underestimate your possibilities to perform at a higher level when challenged.

▶ If you let your initial impressions intimidate you, you're giving your opponent an advantage before the contest even begins. Take a deep breath, and try to emotionally ignore this information. Focus your concentration on yourself and your game preparation. Take care of the things you can control.

One of my best moments in sports came in a high school tennis doubles match. My partner (Terry) and I were facing the first and second singles players from a nearby school, with the winner advancing to the sectionals tournament. We were the clear underdogs. Our opponents walked out onto their home court, dressed like Roger Federer, each carrying two of the best tennis racquets of that time. They were confident, relaxed, and looked every bit the product of many tennis lessons and year-round play. For our part, Terry and I had decent strokes and net games, but we depended more on our general athleticism than grooved groundstrokes.

As the match began, our opponents quickly asserted their dominance. Before long they started acting cocky, joking and carrying on in a disrespectful way. After losing the first set, I remember becoming mad at both our play and our opponent's smug, casual attitude. I turned to Terry and said, "Let's go. We're better than this!" We began to run down every shot, keeping the ball in play, and letting our opponent's overly confident attitude catch up to them. Slowly, the points started going our way. Our play became more aggressive and confident. I can't recall whether I exchanged any words with them, but there were certainly some looks across the net that said, "Okay, let's see what you can do now." As the tide turned, they were unable to recapture their smooth strokes and high level of play. As often happens when the momentum of a game shifts, they began to feel the pressure. We beat them convincingly in the third set to win the match.

Interestingly, I again played one of our opponents in a sectional team playoff a week later. Although he still owned those beautiful strokes, our previous doubles match had destroyed his confidence. I easily beat him in two sets.

Remember that your opponent's apparent excellence is sometimes only a thin veneer covering substantial defects in his or her game. And though you *will* face superior opponents, there are often ways to compensate for your shortcomings. Instead of accepting your supposed disadvantage, relish these challenges and opportunities to succeed. You may create a proud memory that lasts a lifetime.

Pregame Preparation Is Your Responsibility

Besides the mental and physical preparation necessary to compete in your sport (e.g., skills and conditioning), you are also accountable for pregame preparations. These tasks include getting a good night's sleep, eating right, and knowing the "logistics" of where you need to go, when you need to arrive, and how you will get there.

Depending on your age and your living situation, you may have to take a more active role in your game preparation. For example, if your parents work and are not home after school, *you* will need to prepare your own pregame meal before an evening game. If this is the case, make sure that you're eating the right food at the right time (See "Nutrition for athletes" on pg. 21).

You may enjoy staying up later at night, talking on the phone and texting other kids, exploring the Internet, reading, and watching television. If you do not exercise some discipline and reasonably limit these activities, you may not get the amount of sleep you need to perform well in your game the next day.

> 💣 Don't fool yourself or make excuses—you are the one responsible to yourself and your teammates to get your necessary rest.

You should also take responsibility for your rides—knowing when, where and how you will get to your school or other location. Even if you're younger, *you* can still stay on top of your parents to make sure that they get you to the game on time. Your parents are often busy with their many responsibilities and may not place the same emphasis on a timely arrival as you or your coach does.

You're also responsible for the condition of your equipment. Are your shoelaces frayed? If so, replace them so that they don't break during the game. Have you tied double knots (or taped your spikes) so that your shoelaces can't come untied? Look at *all* of your equipment and make sure it's in good shape and properly secured. You don't want any breakdowns during your game that will result in your removal, an embarrassing moment, or any other situation that could cause a problem for your team.

Likewise, check your equipment before practices. No coach likes to have his practice interrupted.

Make sure that you have the *right* equipment to perform at your best. Don't show up to play soccer in your tennis shoes or try to play basketball in shoes that can't grip the floor.

Finally, remember to bring all of your equipment to the game. Lay out everything before packing your sports bag. If your sport or position requires several pieces of equipment, use a checklist. Also, clean your gear after each practice or game and keep it together for the next time. Don't be late because you lost or forgot something!

Although it's easy to always look to your parents to prepare everything for you, try to become more self-reliant and take on responsibility for your game preparations. And what goes for games also goes for practices.

Everyone Fails

At some point or some level, *all* athletes eventually fail. Great players, defined by their last moment heroics, have also succumbed to challenges they could not overcome, obstacles too big, and personal shortcomings of character or performance that resulted in failure. As eloquently expressed in the famous baseball poem, mighty Casey does not always bring joy to Mudville.[5]

Understand that the failure to convert the big shot, and other similar disappointing moments, are a *common bond among all competitive athletes*. Every athlete has experienced the bitter moments of a personal failure or a devastating loss, sometimes forever altered by the event.

One of my more disappointing moments in high school sports occurred playing tennis. My doubles partner and I played a great match to qualify for the sectional tournament, and then easily won our preliminary matches in the sectionals to advance to the finals. Warming up against our opponents, I was confident that we were the better players. Unfortunately, we then played the worst match of our season. We were helpless, flailing away and missing one shot after another. (It was so bad that in one sequence, after I had swung and totally missed a ball at the net, my partner drilled the same ball into the middle of my back!) After shaking hands with our opponents, and walking away, I heaved my racquet into the air in frustration. I couldn't believe we had played so poorly when a good performance might have won the championship.

Failure has different faces. Unlike the above example, sometimes it accompanies your best efforts—those moments when you try to execute a difficult skill or make a key play. Failure (and the unpleasant feelings that go with it) is more likely *when you take greater risks.* But even should you fail, there is still compensation. Putting yourself in the position to take the big shot, and having the courage to do so, is in itself an admirable quality. Regardless of the outcome, these moments reveal a positive aspect of your character—reaching for the prize instead of giving in to a fear of failure. It's not always easy. You will eventually learn, however, that the disappointment of failure is preferable to a lifetime of regret for not facing a challenging moment.

▶ These failures, both real and anticipated, can also have a positive effect. They provide you with the motivation to prepare, giving yourself the best chance to succeed when you face these special moments. Always try to translate any fear of failure that you may have into constructive actions.

Finally, as suggested above, recognize that these types of failure are the necessary flip side of your greatest successes. If you don't try, you'll never enjoy the incredibly satisfying and fulfilling emotion associated with experiencing *your* heroic moment.

Michael Jordan, one of the greatest basketball players of all time, understood this principle well. He failed when, in the midst of a fabulous NBA career, he gave up the sport to pursue his childhood dream of playing professional baseball. And despite his many last second heroics, failure accompanied those other unkind shots that rolled off the rim at the buzzer. Throughout his journey in sports, however, he never stopped trying; he didn't give in to the fear of failing; he wanted the ball in his hands at the end of a close game.

A few years ago, Nike produced an inspirational commercial in which Michael Jordan recounts his failures; it ends with him saying, "I've failed over, and over, and over again in my life, and that is why I succeed." And similarly, on the importance of trying in the face of failure, he once said, "I can accept failure, everyone fails at something. But I can't accept not trying." These words all reflect his competitive attitude.

Embrace your athletic failures as an educational and necessary part of the journey. Know that when you try and fail, you are also experiencing the same set of emotions that all of your sports heroes have gone through. Try to keep both success and failure in its proper perspective. To this point, John Wooden, the famous UCLA basketball coach, said, "Success is never final, failure is never fatal. It's courage that counts."

Knowing When It's Time to Move On

If you're absolutely playing the best you can, but still can't compete, then possibly it's time to consider moving away from playing your sport on an organized, competitive level. *Everyone* faces this moment at some point in their competitive sports lives.

Even the greatest athletes, as they get older, must face their diminished skills and ability to perform. Other talented athletes, full of promise, unfortunately have their careers cut short by injury. Sports mirrors life and reflects both triumphant moments and ones filled with disappointment and regret. When confronted with a major change in your sports life, always remember that your sports heroes have faced (or will face) a similar situation.

Sometimes changes in your physical makeup or athletic skills lead to less success and more stressful situations. What was once fun, is now a chore or an otherwise unpleasant experience.

Early on, I enjoyed success in youth football. I always loved the skill aspect (throwing and catching) of this sport. But as a skinny high school freshman, the physical side of football began to overshadow my limited quarterbacking skills. By my sophomore year, I was relegated to the scout team. Never enjoying physical contact that much, I found myself dreading practices—getting beat-up trying to tackle bigger, stronger teammates.

After our final practice on a cold, wet November day, as I struggled with numbed fingers to untie the laces of my spikes, an overwhelming sense of relief flowed through me. At that moment, I realized that I was going to go home and tell my Dad that I was done playing high school football. What was once a fun, satisfying organized sports experience for me, was no longer so. Change had overtaken me.

Try to recognize whether you're going through similar feelings as you evaluate your personal situation. Although your decision may disappoint your parents or others, stay true to your own feelings. For me, it was a process that took a while—I did not quit simply because I was experiencing some tough times. Instead, I stuck with it until there was a personal moment of full realization that I no longer enjoyed high school football.

Should you reach a similar decision in your life, take comfort in the fact that change often leads to new opportunities (either in sports or other areas of your life).

A few weeks after my last football season ended, during basketball tryouts and practices, I found that I was now quicker than many of my teammates. I started on the junior varsity team that year and my success in basketball continued through high school and into college. One door closed and another opened.

▶ If you still enjoy your sport, don't give in too easily to disappointment and frustration—you may only have reached a temporary roadblock or performance plateau. Everyone gets knocked down. One of the defining characteristics of all successful athletes is their ability to get back up and try again. Persistence can still lead to success.

▶ If you're questioning whether you want to continue playing a sport, first look at whether you still enjoy it. And if not, then ask yourself why.

A Final Word on Competing

Competition in sports is fun—as long as you believe you *can* compete. You may be a vast underdog. But if you believe there's a chance to win, competing becomes an exciting challenge. Learning a sport's fundamental skills, practicing these skills, and picking the right sport and level of competition, all help instill this belief in you.

Competition also can bring out the best in you, spurring moments of unexpected grace and heroism. For some, these flashes of perfection are spiritual. In any case, knowing you've competed to the best of your ability provides you with an inner satisfaction that is, in and of itself, a prize.

So take a chance. Give it your all. As Wayne Gretzky, arguably the greatest hockey player of all time, said, "You'll always miss 100% of the shots you don't take."

Finally, consider one last benefit of competing: competition engenders respect between competitors—sometimes even deep friendships. The strong bonds of friendship between Larry Bird and Earvin "Magic" Johnson arose out of their shared, intense competitions in both college and professional basketball.

Many years ago, the famous track star Jesse Owens reflected on this positive aspect of competition, and said, "Friendships born on the field of athletic strife are the real gold of competition. Awards become corroded, friends gather no dust." These words recognize that competition often unites opponents who pursue common goals and aspirations. Experiences shared, ones that bring out the best in you and your opponents, forge a unique, lasting bond—for each appreciates the other's role in helping shape their excellence.

▶ Appreciate both the internal rewards (friendships, inner satisfaction) and the external ones (awards, recognition) that arise from competing in sports.

138

What Your
Coach Wants

*I really want to make the varsity team this
year. How can I improve my chances?*

... Ben

To succeed in competitive sports you must discover the sports
you enjoy and can play well. Along the way, you need to
maximize your physical ability, learn and develop the necessary
sports skills, and gain an understanding of how and when to apply
these skills during a contest.

You will also need to pay attention to what your coaches want.
These individuals are the gatekeepers to your success. They are your
teachers. They are the ones who evaluate your ability (both existing
and potential) along with your capacity to play a team role. They
control your playing time and often determine your fate in competitive organized sports.

Most coaches in competitive programs are interested in developing their kids both as successful individuals and athletes. They also
want to win. In pursuing this goal, they select the mix of players
that provide the best chance to do so. Coaches always seek athletes
with a natural talent for playing a sport. But good coaches also

recognize and value the more subtle, less athletic "talents" that can enable a young person to play an important role on the team.

You need to understand these principles in your efforts to secure more playing time. And if you want to maximize your chances of success, you need to know how coaches think and what they are looking for.

How a Coach Builds a Team

A good coach knows that team success always begins with the players. Their abilities, both realized and potential, are the raw material from which the coach molds a successful team.

Every coach would love to have a team comprised of equally talented superstars—players able and willing to do it all. But that's not how it works. At all levels of play, the reality is that each coach must put together a team from individuals who have different strengths and weaknesses.

So how does a coach go about this task? He or she starts by evaluating and selecting players and then moves on to developing each one's ability. Team roles are established and the coach's system implemented.

Match players with team roles

A coach first needs to find players who can play the *team roles* necessary for the team to succeed. These roles can be viewed from the perspective of *playing a position* (point guard, quarterback, pitcher, etc.) or meeting a team's *functional need* (scorer, defender, ball-handler).

With the right mix of players (ones who can play the required team roles well), a team can successfully compete—even against teams comprised of superior individual athletes.

Identify athleticism, skills, potential, and intangibles

In evaluating prospective players, and the team roles they can play, a coach considers a variety of player attributes. Each player presents an observable body type, athletic quality, and set of sports skills. Athleticism and body type are often invaluable qualities necessary to a team's success (and ones that can't be taught). Similarly, excellent sports skills are important. Less obvious is a young athlete's development potential and other more intangible attributes.

Although coaches need to have players who can immediately perform well, coaches are also interested in young athletes who may develop into exceptional players. For example, having just gone through a growth spurt, a young boy or girl may play a sport in an awkward, less-coordinated manner. But to a perceptive eye, the player's movements and skills also demonstrate an underlying quality that suggests the player will soon "grow" into his or her body.

A coach is also interested in players who demonstrate leadership, perseverance, a competitive nature, and other less tangible traits. These coupled with other valuable attributes, such as a player's attitude, willingness to prepare, and attention to detail all factor into a coach's player evaluation.

Develop individual and team skills (improve the parts)

Once a coach has selected the team's players, he continues to build the team by helping players develop both their individual and team skills. As the players' abilities improve, the coach considers whether their team roles are still appropriate. (A player's team role can evolve—even within the current season.)

Match systems and players (improve the whole)

Finally, a coach puts in place his or her team strategies and tactics—plugging in players that best fit his or her system while also modifying the system to better fit the players' unique set of abilities.

Here's a diagram that summarizes the general process that coaches follow in building a team:

Building a Team

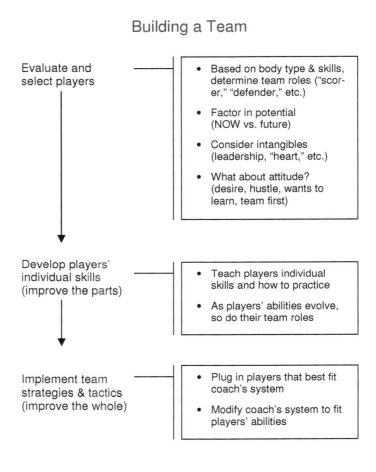

Evaluate and select players
- Based on body type & skills, determine team roles ("scorer," "defender," etc.)
- Factor in potential (NOW vs. future)
- Consider intangibles (leadership, "heart," etc.)
- What about attitude? (desire, hustle, wants to learn, team first)

Develop players' individual skills (improve the parts)
- Teach players individual skills and how to practice
- As players' abilities evolve, so do their team roles

Implement team strategies & tactics (improve the whole)
- Plug in players that best fit coach's system
- Modify coach's system to fit players' abilities

Finding Your Team Role

This reliance on roles to achieve team success is what opens many opportunities for lesser athletes with limited skill sets. It can also be *your* door to success in sports. To find your possible team roles, ask yourself three questions:

1. What strategies and tactics are favored by my coach?

2. What roles are needed within this style of play?

3. What are my strengths and weaknesses?

As you consider each of these questions and formulate your answers, try to see where the answers overlap. By targeting the right roles, you can improve your chance to make a team, gain more minutes, and play in a way that's appreciated by both your teammates and coach.

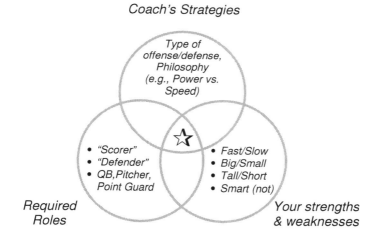

For instance, in football, a coach may prefer a run-first version of a "spread" offense. In contrast to a "pro" offense that requires a quarterback who is an excellent drop-back passer, this spread offense needs a quarterback who is first a good runner. Likewise, it may require more mobile lineman. The emphasis is placed on lineman who are quicker, have good feet, and can get downfield or to the outside to block their opponent. In this case, size and strength are less important than speed and agility.

Now, where would you and your unique set of characteristics possibly fit in the above example? If you do not possess good hand-eye coordination, or outstanding size and weight—but you're quick, intelligent, and like contact—you might target playing the offensive line position in a spread offense.

> ▶ Each coach has a unique view on what mix of players, strategies, and tactics leads to success. To help you evaluate and understand where you possibly fit in, don't hesitate to ask your coaches where they believe your opportunity lies.

Of course, the ideal setting that best matches your abilities may not exist. (In the above example, your high school's football coach may run an offense that's based on a more traditional power-running game.) But you should try to understand where your unique attributes best fit in and whether a certain position or role is one that you would possibly enjoy playing.

Excelling in a defensive team role is an avenue to success for many players who have limited sports skills—especially in smaller schools with fewer athletes. This role is one that depends to a large degree on a player's desire, hustle, focus, and other attributes related more to the mind than the body. A good defender is appreciated in virtually every team sport and by most coaches.

In high school, I played varsity basketball for a coach who preferred an aggressive man-to-man defensive scheme. He appreciated players who hustled and could defend their man well. My junior year, having only limited offensive skills, I concentrated on playing excellent defense—both in practice and in games. I wanted to shut down my opponent. This defensive role was the one in which I could contribute to my team, get more playing time, and eventually leverage to become a starter.

> ▶ When you apply the above approach to **all** of the sports available to you, the possibilities expand for you to find the right role within the right sport.

Primary team roles

Every team sport requires excellence in primary roles. These are the ones which are crucial to a team's ability to compete.

In basketball, most successful teams require quality play at the point guard and low post positions. A successful basketball team also typically requires that someone play the important functional role of "scorer." A pro football team's most important role is the quarterback. Baseball games are more often won by the team that has excellent pitchers. Soccer, hockey, and lacrosse teams need a forward who can score and a goalie who can defend.

Failure at these key positions can doom a team's chances for success, negating any advantage the team may have at other positions. For instance, a basketball team that lacks a guard to bring the ball up the court against a pressure defense will rarely have the opportunity to get the ball to its outstanding big men.

These primary roles tend to go to the better athletes and individuals who possess exceptionally strong sports skills that match the requirements of the associated position. Through diligent training and effort, however, less talented athletes can sometimes succeed in these primary roles.

If you're expecting to play one of these key positions, understand that you will need to show your coach that you have the required talent and skills.

Secondary team roles

While there are only a few primary team roles available, there are *many* secondary roles. You should understand that these secondary roles are essential to a team's success. Understand also, that almost every coach appreciates this truth.

These roles encompass all the "little" things that lead to a team's success. Examples of functional team roles include "defender," "ball-handler," "rebounder," and "utility man."

Again, try to identify any attributes you possess that can lead to success in one of your sport's secondary roles. If you have a stubborn, persistent nature, are reasonably quick, and possess good endurance you may find success in the defender role discussed above. If you lack outstanding

💣 Playing a secondary role well only takes you so far. If you're missing an essential skill, it's less likely you will find success playing that sport. Leverage your strengths to secure your position, but work on your weaknesses to expand it.

athleticism, but have the ability to accurately focus on and consistently hit a target, you may still find success as a "shooter" (spot-up shooter in basketball, football place-kicker, etc.).

Each player who plays a secondary role benefits from having the ability to additionally play other roles. For example, a basketball player who is an outstanding defender, but is also a good passer and threat to score, provides more value to a team (and its coach).

Remember that coaches are *always* looking to find players to fill team roles.

Your role can change

As you mature and improve your skills, the team role you play often changes. Where once you played a minor secondary role you now play a more important one. You may even find yourself playing a primary team role.

A *physical change* can suddenly provide you with the ability to excel in an entirely different role or position. For example, the middle school volleyball setter who gains a foot in height after puberty may become a hitter on his high school volleyball team.

Skill development can also lead to a different team role. A basketball shooting guard, for instance, may work hard to improve his or her ball-handling skills and evolve into an outstanding point guard.

Your role may also change as you move to higher levels of competition. Where you once were the outstanding athlete and scorer, you may now play a secondary role. Be prepared to adapt, especially when you first move to a higher level.

Good coaches constantly evaluate their players' ability and skills. They realize that individual player development is a path to improving their team's likelihood for success.

💣 Don't undersell your abilities or lose yourself in a role that doesn't fit you. Coaches expect you to play up to your talent level and will become irritated with a player who does not do so. An athletic player who has the ability to score, but regularly passes up open shots and other scoring opportunities, will only succeed in frustrating the team's coach.

Coaches Have Different Perspectives

Coaches possess their own unique perspectives on how their sport should be played and the associated skills and values they need to teach.

One coach may prefer a man-to-man defense while another one is convinced that a zone defense is best. But besides different views on strategy and game tactics, your coaches may also hold entirely different philosophical views on what constitutes success and how to achieve it. You need to understand the type of coach you play for.

To one extreme, your coach may view success largely as a matter of winning versus losing. This type of coach will believe that players should dedicate themselves to the team, work hard, and sacrifice to reach the primary goal of winning as many games as possible. Your coach will likely invest a great amount of time into the program and expect you to do the same. You're more likely to play for this type of coach as you climb the competitive ladder.

Toward the other end of the spectrum is the coach who believes that players should have fun, enjoy the game, while also learning skills and possibly life lessons. This coach may or may not invest a large amount of effort in his program. He or she is less concerned about you winning and more so about you playing to the best of your ability, and striving to improve. You are more likely to play for this type of coach in youth programs when you're younger.

▶ If you're playing for a hard-nosed, demanding coach, you will have to put in the necessary extra time expected of you. If your coach is intense, display a similar attitude (as opposed to one that is more laid-back). Pay close attention to what parts of the game your coach emphasizes and concentrate on improving your play in those areas.

Typically you will have little control over who is your coach— especially if you're an average athlete playing at the more competitive levels.

▶ Focus on your coach's perception of what's important, not your own!

You may prefer a prior coach's style or approach, but this is irrelevant to your current situation.

If you want to maximize your opportunity to play, you need to adapt your preparation and play to match your coach's perspective and needs. His perception of you may be very different from your own. For example, you may think that you're an asset to your team when the ball is in your hands and you're aggressively trying to score. But your coach may instead see you as a liability—a selfish player who won't pass the ball to an open teammate.

💣 Coaches sometimes adapt their coaching style to better match a player's particular personality type and attitude—but you shouldn't expect this to happen. Unless you demonstrate some unique talent, it's unlikely you will be chosen over someone who more closely fits your coach's model player.

Tryouts

Since you're investing time in reading this book, it's likely that you want to play better in more competitive settings. It's also likely that one of your goals is to "make" a high school, club, or AAU team. You may even hope to play in college or beyond. In all of these settings, you are competing against others for a spot on the team. And that means you will need to go through an evaluation process. You will need to "try out."

How can you improve your chances to make a team? As already discussed, understanding the team roles you can play well is essential. Doing the things that your coach perceives as important is also helpful. (Reread the topics above!)

But let's take a closer look at a tryout, what you can expect, and the ways in which you can improve your chances of getting picked.

Start by doing some preparation. Make sure that you understand the format of the tryouts, their scheduled time and place. Obviously, you want to show up on time, with the right gear, and ready to play.

Well before the tryout, you may have the opportunity to talk with some other players who have played for the current coach. Ask questions so that you have some idea of what to expect in the tryout. Use this information. Modify your practice preparation to emphasize any skills or physical abilities that your coach values. For example, if your coach stresses physical conditioning and expects his or her players to come to tryouts in shape, make sure that you train accordingly. Regardless of your overall ability, you don't want to be gasping for air, while others continue to effortlessly run and play. Make sure that your training program is well-matched to your sport. If your sport requires bursts of speed over short distances, duplicate those conditions by including lots of sprints in your training program.

Disregard your first impressions

Unless you're one of the top players, tryouts can be intimidating. When you arrive and look around, you will see other players that seemingly look better than you. Some are bigger and stronger. Some are faster or lightning-quick. Others have impressive ball skills that look more polished than yours. Still other players will appear to have nice shots and an ability to score.

But you should always remember that playing a sport well involves much more than simply having an outstanding physical attribute or a few excellent skills. Your coach knows this, and he or she is looking for a blend of qualities in you that will add value to his or her team.

So don't worry a lot about what you see around you. Much of what first appears is illusion. During drills and actual play, each player's true strengths and weaknesses are gradually exposed. Many of those who first impress have their own set of ugly warts.

Focus on your own play

So what do you do to improve your chances to make the team? Focus on your own play! Trust your skills and preparation. Play in the moment, and don't worry about things you can't control. Do what *you* do well!

If your strengths are in areas that you believe are important to your coach, look for opportunities to demonstrate them. For instance, are you a good defender? If so, seek man-to-man match-ups where you are defending one of the better scorers—preferably one that you believe your coach holds in high regard. Shut them down. Make it obvious to your coach that you excel in this part of the game.

In the rest of this chapter we will discuss many of the player attributes that coaches appreciate. Not only do they apply to gaining more minutes of playing time, but also are ones that will help you make a team. These include preparedness, effort, listening and learning, avoiding mental mistakes, doing the little things, and leadership and other intangibles. During tryouts, *always* look for opportunities to demonstrate these qualities.

Learning your fate

Whether it's a phone call, a personal meeting with the coach or a posted list of who made the team, learning your fate is an emotional moment. Exhilaration or disappointment likely awaits you. No one likes being rejected, and you may also experience some fear of rejection. Remember that every player faces rejection at some point in their career.

If you don't make the team, try to stay positive—especially if you're young. You may still be physically maturing. Likewise, your skills may be at an early stage of development. Ask the coach what he or she believes are your strengths and weaknesses. Find out where you specifically need to improve. Ask the coach what team role may provide an opportunity for you to make the team next year.

Things change each year. Older players move on and some quit or focus on another sport. If you love playing your sport, keep playing pickup and in other leagues. You just may make that team next year!

Are You Prepared?

One of the personal characteristics that coaches appreciate in their players is a *desire to prepare*. Good preparation in competitive sports starts in the off-season when players train their bodies and work to improve their skills.

This preparation may occur through playing another sport. When selecting secondary sports to play in high school, you should consider how these sports supplement your primary sport. Do they provide you with the physical conditioning that is complementary to your favorite sport? Similarly, do these other sports help you develop or cross-train skills that will improve performance in your primary sport? For example, a football lineman might want to consider wrestling in the winter to better develop his sense of leverage and hand-to-hand skills. A basketball player might choose volleyball to improve two-footed jumping and visuospatial skills.

Some players choose to focus entirely on training and skill development specific to the player's primary sport. This approach may mean lifting weights in the off-season to gain weight and strength. Time spent with a personal trainer may help these players develop or improve sports specific skills. And some players continue to play their sport year-round in club or AAU leagues.

💣 While training in the off-season, be watchful for signs of burn-out (apathy toward playing your sport). Also, you may be more susceptible to "overuse" injuries when you play a single sport year-round.

But whatever off-season training choices you make, coaches expect that you will arrive for the beginning of the season and tryouts in excellent physical condition.

Preparation is also important during your season. Do you get enough sleep, eat right, and otherwise take care of your body so you're prepared to practice and play your best? Do you take care of your other responsibilities (schoolwork) so that they do not interfere with your participation in sports? Do you listen to your coach's instruction and review new plays on your own afterwards?

More often than not, your play will reflect your preparedness. And the better you play the more valuable you are to your coach and teammates.

Are You Giving Your Best Effort?

All coaches value players who hustle and give their best effort. Although effort is not a substitute for skill, it's often the difference between two players with similar skills.

This is especially true in the secondary roles necessary to a team's success. The "defender," who through sheer determination, desire, and effort plays great defense, is one example. A "rebounder" in basketball, who despite a smaller stature pursues every rebound with anticipation and tenacity, is another.

> ▶ Coaches **want** to choose the player who gives 100%. Make their choice an easier one!

Effort, desire, and hustle are qualities you directly control. Use this to your advantage in pursuing more playing time or a spot on your team's roster. (The upcoming section "Focus on what you control" discusses this behavior in more detail.)

Listen, Learn, and Pay Attention to Detail

A good coach is a good teacher. Likewise, a good player is a good student.

Coaches expect players to listen closely to their instruction; they expect players to learn the lessons taught. Just as you need to live in the moment when you're playing, focus on your coach's instruction and don't let your mind drift. Look at your coach; be respectful. If you're confused, ask questions.

Coaches spend a great deal of time teaching their players skills, plays, and concepts. Throughout this instruction, coaches will stress specific actions (in particular situations) that players *must* always do.

Should you fail to do so, you're committing a *mental mistake*. When you forget a play assignment, your position, or who you're guarding, you are guilty of making this type of mistake. Coaches are usually much less tolerant of these types of mistakes than physical ones (e.g., dribbling a basketball off your foot, failing to convert an easy shot). They view mental mistakes as a failure on your part to listen, learn, and pay attention to detail—all behaviors under your control. When these mistakes occur in situations discussed by your coach, possibly ones emphasized in practice, you are setting yourself up for reduced playing time.

💣 Most coaches are less tolerant of mental mistakes. Make these too often and you will quickly find yourself on the bench.

As a basketball coach, one of my pet peeves is when experienced players, lined up for an opponent's free throw, fail to box out the shooter. When this happens, the shooter can rebound the ball and sometimes score. Despite telling my players the importance of communicating to each other who will box out the shooter, they sometimes forget to go through this process. As the players line up, I find myself continually yelling, "Who's got the shooter?!"

An important task like the above one is entirely controllable by you, the player on the floor. It's about paying attention to detail and avoiding mistakes. Make sure that you understand your responsibilities as they relate to specific game situations and your coach's expectations. Follow through on your responsibilities, performing the necessary tasks and procedures every time. Continually think and evaluate the situation. Where am I? What's the score? Where should I and my teammates be positioned? What information should I be communicating to my teammates?

Avoiding mental mistakes and taking care of the small details is often as important as executing a physical skill. Show your coach that your head is in the game. If you want more playing time, don't have your coach pointing at you from the sideline and screaming, "Who's got the shooter?!"

153

Minimize Mistakes

As discussed above, players who *avoid* mental mistakes usually find favor with their coach. When coupled with reasonable skills, minimizing mistakes can provide you with a competitive advantage—both against your opponent and when competing for a position on your team.

Casey Stengel, a successful baseball manager for the New York Yankees many years ago, once said, "Most games are lost, not won." He was referring to the idea that more often than not, teams beat themselves by committing too many mistakes. In his experience, fielding errors, poor base-running, hanging a curveball, chasing bad pitches, and other fundamental mistakes lost more games than exceptional play (e.g., home runs) won games.

Think about how this coaching perspective relates to your game. Do you put your team at a disadvantage by making too many mistakes? Even if you're naturally gifted, do your mistakes outweigh your "home runs"?

Try to minimize your mistakes without being fearful of making them. To play a sport well, you often need to push your play to the edge of your abilities—but you need to know where that edge is. You need to know when to back off and when to go for it. You need to balance your play to become the consistent performer your coach wants and needs.

Self-awareness, practice repetitions, and game experience will all help you find this balance. Also listen to constructive criticism from your coach and others you trust. They can alert you to possible problems with your play and also provide instruction that will help you eliminate recurring mental and physical mistakes.

Why's That Kid Screaming "I'm Open, I'm Open!"?

In team sports, communicating with other players is a positive player trait. But nothing says that you're a beginner more than when you regularly stand still, wave your hands, and scream to your teammates "I'm open! I'm open!" This behavior is typical of most young players (first through third grade). Their limited understanding of the game is centered upon what they do when the ball is in their hands. Since that's where the fun is, they want the ball.

Unfortunately, older players sometimes fall into this same behavior. They may not yell or wave their hands as often, but they still stand in one place until someone passes them the ball.

Stop shouting and do something—MOVE! Go set a screen. Clear out space. Focus some of your attention on the potential action and opportunities *away* from the ball. Consider what you can do to help a teammate NOW.

When you do something without the ball to help a teammate score, you're also more likely to get a pass from that person. And when others on your team begin to play with this unselfish attitude and style, the passing and scoring opportunities increase, everyone is involved, and the fun really begins. You find yourself part of a ballet of movement and interactions that can lead to perfect moments of anticipation, execution, and improvisation.

There are times when you will want to stay in position—most typically when you're part of a specific offensive set or play, or playing a position within a team defense. You may also individually decide to maintain a position to create space between yourself and other players. In some cases, your team's needs and your offensive talent may dictate that you look to score more often than your teammates. But unless you have a specific responsibility, move and create opportunities for your teammates.

So if you want to look like a beginner, go ahead, stand around and yell, "I'm open!" You may actually get a few more opportunities with the ball. But your coach will notice this behavior, and possibly judge you less favorably.

If you want to look like you know what you're doing, and help your team succeed, move without the ball and do the other little things that create opportunities for you and your teammates.

Leadership and Other "Intangibles"

As mentioned in the beginning of this chapter, coaches evaluate players both on their observable traits (athleticism, sports skills, body type) and less-obvious ones. This latter category includes several of the qualities already discussed (attitude, willingness to learn and prepare, and attention to detail).

Even less apparent are those special qualities that only a few players on a team typically possess—the ability to perform at a high level in pressure situations (a "clutch" player), a "never give up" mind-set (a player with "heart"), and the over-arching quality of leadership. Players who demonstrate these qualities not only contribute to their team's success by their own play, but also by the way in which they affect their teammate's play. Their character inspires others to reach higher and, in turn, give their best effort.

Leadership comes in various forms and is earned—by your play, the quality of your character, or more often by both. You can lead simply by the example you set. If you play at a high level, and within the framework of team play, you will gain the respect of your teammate. You don't need to give "rah-rah" speeches. Your teammates will naturally look to you to lead them in difficult circumstances. And when you do talk, others will listen.

Self-confidence is always present in players who lead by example. They believe in themselves and their abilities. Coaches love players who are confident—but only if the confidence is well-placed.

Several years ago, while I was coaching a team in a middle school basketball game, the official called a technical foul on our opponent. As I was pointing to one of my better ninth graders to take the shots, another boy, only in seventh grade, came over to me and said, "Coach, if you let me

▶ Although you may not possess charisma or the ability to lead by athletic example, you can still show leadership in smaller ways. How do you react when your team is struggling? Do you go "quietly into the night" or do you challenge yourself and your teammates to be better? ("We're better than this—let's go!")

shoot, I'll make both of them." He was a good young player, but I was more impressed with his confidence and bold prediction. I decided to let him take the technical free throws. He went to the line and calmly sank the first shot, and then the second. But what happened next was even better. He walked by me, gave me a big smile, and without saying a word returned to the court. I was impressed with this boy's quiet self-confidence. How could any coach not be?

Leadership is also a byproduct of a noble character. If despite a lack of outstanding ability, you give your best effort, are willing to sacrifice your individual accomplishments when necessary for the team's benefit, and otherwise demonstrate admirable character traits such as courage and honesty, your teammates will follow your lead.

Obviously, coaches would prefer all of their players to have outstanding talent, confidence, character, and the ability to lead others when needed. But the reality is that most players are flawed. Team roles need to be filled. You may find, despite your lack of outstanding athleticism, that your abilities are sufficient to play an important role on your team. And in doing so, you may also find that you possess leadership skills that are highly valued by your coach.

Focus on What You Can Control

I often run into youth players I've coached who have grown up and are of high school age. I usually ask them how they are doing and whether they're still playing. If I know they are on a high school team, I'll ask whether they're enjoying the experience.

I'm always a little disappointed when I hear a young athlete I've coached tell me: "I don't get along with the coach." Unfortunately, these words are the usual outward sign of a boy or girl who is starting to lose ground to other players or otherwise feels frustrated with their playing situation. Blaming the coach is an easier way for many struggling players to deflect personal shortcomings or failure.

Before you throw in the towel...

If I know that a player has good skills, or sense that the player still wants to succeed despite their frustration, I tell these young athletes to refocus their energies on actions and behaviors that *every* coach likes—behaviors that the player controls. As already discussed, there are opportunities in most sports to succeed based in large part on a player's desire, attention to detail, and willingness to sacrifice personal goals for those of the team.

▶ Let your practice and play demonstrate, in no uncertain terms, why the coach must play you more. Regardless of other factors (e.g., personality, parents and politics), almost all coaches will play their best players.

Consider how you can apply the above traits to your sport. In basketball, you might first look to focus on your defense, raising your intensity level. Hustle. Hit the floor. Use practice as an opportunity to shut down the player you're covering, preferably one with whom you are competing. Every team needs a star defender. For other parts of your game, concentrate on the little things such as making the pass to the open man, reducing mistakes and turnovers, and consistently boxing out your opponent to improve you're rebounding. Make the coach ask himself, "How does he get so many rebounds for a player his size?" You want the coach to recognize your "intangibles"—the less obvious characteristics that make you a winner. Most team sports contain the same or similar situations and opportunities to succeed.

Coaches always appreciate players who embody these types of qualities. When faced with selecting between two players of equal physical ability, a coach will choose the one that demonstrates these characteristics. Don't be the other person!

Don't Talk with Mom and Dad in the Stands

You and your parents may have a close connection when it comes to sports. One or both of your parents may have taken an active role in your development. They may have coached you in youth sports.

As a result, they may shout out instructions from the stands. They may try to engage you in a two-way conversation. The problem with this behavior is that it diverts your attention from game situations and your coach's instruction.

> 💣 Engaging in this behavior also suggests that a player may be overly concerned with how others judge him or her—a self-esteem issue that can have more serious consequences outside of sports.

If you're playing in a competitive organized sport, especially at the high school level, understand that coaches *universally* dislike this behavior. They want you to focus either on your play or their instructions. They don't want to compete with your parents for your attention.

Similarly, keep your pre-game interactions with friends in the stands to a minimum. Concentrate on the task at hand. Talk with your parents and friends *after* the game is over.

Are You the (Bad) Apple of Your Coach's Eye?

Coaches approach each season with specific goals in mind. Besides assembling a team of individuals that provide the best chance to win games, coaches have a strategy to develop their team over the course of the season. The primary means to develop both the players and team are the team's practices.

Sometimes a coach is confronted with a player whose behavior repeatedly disrupts practices. This player may talk while the coach is talking, mock other players (or the coach), execute drills half-heartedly, or constantly joke around. This type of behavior is often contagious and can sometimes ruin practices.

Most coaches in competitive programs will not put up with any of the above behavior. Where your misconduct is more serious, you can expect to either sit the bench or be dismissed from the team.

Some coaches may be more tolerant of their "star" players. But either way, you do not help yourself (or your team) by acting in an irresponsible or disrespectful manner.

Coaches may also have team policies that are mandatory. You may not agree with them, but most coaches will hold you to these standards.

A well-known example occurred years ago between Bill Walton, the All-American basketball center from UCLA, and his legendary coach, John Wooden. Despite Coach Wooden's policy prohibiting facial hair, Bill showed up for practice one day sporting a beard. When Coach Wooden asked him about his beard, Bill stated that he felt it was his right to have facial hair. Coach Wooden said, "Bill, I respect a man who has strong beliefs and is willing to stand up for them...and the team is going to miss you." Not surprisingly, a shaven Bill Walton showed up for practice the next day! [6]

💣 Playing sports on your high school or college team is a privilege, not a right. You risk forfeiting a valuable life experience if you behave in a way that is detrimental to your team or your coach's expectations. If you choose to oppose the coach (even for a good reason), you risk dismissal. Weigh your choices carefully.

Evaluating a Player

PART III:

Your Path
in Sports

Take a Look at Yourself in the Mirror

I love playing sports but am heavier and slower than a lot of other guys on my team. I'm thinking of quitting, but want to know if there's any hope for me to get better?

... Tom

What's your first memory of playing sports? Possibly it was throwing a ball around with your mom or dad. Maybe it was a game of kickball during your first gym class in elementary school. Or perhaps it was when your parents signed you up for your first Little League baseball, youth football, or soccer team.

Not long afterwards, it's likely that one of your friends came up with the idea of organizing your own game. With other kids in your neighborhood, you joined together to play a game of "pickup" baseball, basketball, football, soccer, hockey, or some other sport.

Depending on the type of neighborhood you lived in, the game was played in a backyard, street, playground, or an empty field.

During these early experiences playing sports, you may have also faced your first real moment of self-judgment and asked yourself, "How good am I compared to the other kids playing?" For some of you the answer was not a positive one. Looking into the mirror, you may not have liked what you saw.

As it relates to sports, your self-perception is based on several factors. Of these, confidence in your innate athletic ability stands out. If you seem to possess natural athleticism, it's likely you will have a positive view of yourself and playing sports. If not, you may hold a more pessimistic view. But consider also that your perception of what it takes to achieve success in sports may be distorted. You may be unaware that there are paths to success in sports that do not depend solely on athleticism. You may even have a mistaken perception of what "success" actually is.

If you're a beginner or less athletic novice struggling to fit in with others, this chapter will help you better understand how your physical abilities, body type, and other personal qualities all affect your opportunity to succeed playing sports. Along the way, you will also discover approaches to playing more effectively.

Paths to Success

Success in sports comes in different forms. The most obvious one is derived from your ability to play a sport well. You win. Your team wins. Everyone wants to play with you.

How do you become one of these players?

The best athletes are usually gifted with "natural" athletic talent. They typically have physical attributes (size, strength, speed) that set them apart from others. They may also have exceptional motor skills (hand-eye coordination).

But here's an essential truth you need to understand: *natural talent alone does not determine success in sports.* Although it often accompanies success, it's only one ingredient in the mix of qualities that define a winning, competitive athlete. As previously discussed, hard work (practice and preparation) is also necessary to shape one's talent into effective play. Likewise, good coaching and instruction help transform raw talent into a more refined product. Other more intangible qualities also play an important role. The "will-to-win," ability to learn, and tactical intelligence, all help define an athlete's prospects for success.

▶ Although natural talent helps one excel at playing sports, it's not a prerequisite for success. There are other ways for an athlete with less talent to succeed—ones that an athlete can learn and control.

You should also appreciate that *talent isn't absolute—it grows or shrinks relative to circumstance.* In youth, it's often relative to one's physical development. You may physically mature earlier or later than others your age. "Stars" at the youth level may dominate because they are bigger, taller, or stronger. But like runners who charge to the front at the start of a long race, only to quickly fall back into the pack, their advantage is frequently short-lived. No longer tall or strong for their age as they and others mature, their talent (in this case a physical advantage) disappears.

The measure of one's talent is also *relative to the level of competition.* Middle school stars who possess outstanding skills may find that this talent alone isn't the path to success when they graduate to high school. Many others may now have similar abilities—ones that were regarded as exceptional at lower levels.

Consider professional athletes. At lower levels, most were exceptionally gifted athletes. But at the elite professional level, many are now viewed as having limited athleticism. Their talent is less remarkable.

Yet despite their diminished relative ability, many of these professional players still enjoy great success. For example, from 2006 through 2008, a decidedly non-athletic Jason Kapono found success in the NBA because of his ability to make 3-point shots. Tom Brady did not become one of the best quarterbacks of all time because he is a physically great athlete. (His NFL combine results, including a 5.28 40 yard time, were some of the worst ever recorded for a quarterback.) Instead, he adapted his play at the professional level to counter the quicker, faster, and stronger NFL defenders. He learned how to more quickly process patterns of play and make the right decisions.

These players all find other ways to play their sport well; their path to success changes. They may excel in one area of play—possibly one that is crucial to the success of their team. They build upon their experience and countless practice repetitions; their minds have a fuller grasp of how to play the game, enabling them to more quickly take advantage of opportunities that present themselves during a contest. They may also have greater mental discipline to both prepare and persevere. They're better conditioned. They work and play harder. Their will to win is strong.

If you're a young athlete who wants to play competitive sports, your path to success will likely resemble the one just described. Few athletes consistently win throughout their career by relying on their athletic talent alone. Instead, hard work and the other qualities described above come into play. And this is good news for you and every other young athlete. You *can* develop and control many of these other qualities!

The Successful Athlete—a Mix of Qualities

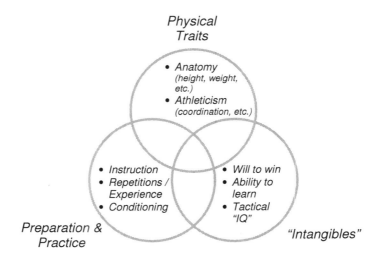

168

More on Success

Although many view success in sports through the lens of winning and losing contests, "making" a team, and possibly becoming a star player, there's another way in which to view success. It's less obvious, but one that nevertheless provides you with numerous personal benefits—many of which will continue paying dividends throughout your life.

This other view is one that embodies the concept that "success" is about finding personal fulfillment. It's about being the best you can be and enjoying the act of playing itself. This approach to playing sports is one that can potentially enrich *every* participant's life.

▶ Whether pursuing excellence in sports or other areas of your life, *be the best you can be.* Or as Abraham Lincoln put it, "Whatever you are, be a good one."

Yes, it's nice to gain the recognition associated with making your high school team or becoming its star player. But sports offer much more than accolades and attention.

Sports can lead to great friendships that last a lifetime. They can provide you with a sense of community and camaraderie—bonding with others in pursuit of winning a glorious contest—whether it's in the backyard or in front of a large crowd. Sports help connect you to that part of you that just wants to RUN. They combine strategy, skill, and physical effort in a single, *fun* package. Sports help improve your physical fitness and self esteem—creating a healthy balance between your physical and intellectual selves. Sports can provide you with a means of creative expression.

Even lacking the ability to play competitive sports at higher levels, you can still pursue a path in sports that enhances the quality of your life. Not just now, but throughout your life.

Finally, you should also realize that your gifts, talent, and path to success may lie outside of sports. You may prefer playing a musical instrument, acting in your school's plays, pursuing academic excellence, or participating in any number of enjoyable, worthwhile activities. What's important is that you follow a path that serves to reveal *your* passions and purpose in life. Maybe it's a life full of playing sports—maybe not.

Frogs Can Become Princes

Things change. Sometimes it's not a lot of fun dealing with change. All of a sudden, you're too small, too big, too slow, too awkward, or too shy. Some part of you is different and sets you apart from others. Different doesn't seem better at certain ages.

But one truth prevails—change provides opportunity. And this fact applies to sports as much as any other part of life. As your body and mind develop, new opportunities to succeed in sports present themselves while past competitive advantages fall to the wayside. Each year brings new possibilities.

▶ Change often arrives suddenly; you may unexpectedly find yourself performing on a different level. Try to recognize these moments. If the changes remove a competitive advantage, look at other ways to compensate. If the change is positive, adjust your expectations upward and develop your newfound advantage.

As a high school sophomore, trying out for the junior varsity basketball team, I entertained few thoughts of finding any great success. The year before, I was a seldom used substitute on my freshman team and had just finished a miserable football season. I hoped simply to make the JV team.

But during tryouts and the first practices, I noticed that something was different. I was able to often dribble past my defenders and score. On defense, I frustrated my opponents by consistently shutting them down. I began to realize that I was much quicker than the year before.

After one of these early practices, I recall walking behind a group of teammates back to the locker room and overhearing one of the prior year's starters worriedly confide to another, "Rhoads is looking pretty good; I think he may start." He was right—I started every game that year. The physical changes I underwent as my body matured made me more competitive.

Whatever your physical limitations are now, try to maximize your skills, stay positive, and don't give up. If you're fortunate, physical changes will drive a dramatic, natural improvement in your ability to play a sport.

For others, the changes will be more modest, but still provide new opportunities to excel. As your body changes, you may find yourself playing a different position or role on your team. Skills that were average in one position can become exceptional in another. Too slow as a football running back, you're now considered quick for your new larger size and position as a lineman. To the opposite, although you're still "too small," you are now quicker than the players who have grown.

▶ Play multiple sports (and different positions) when you're young. Learning a variety of sports skills helps provide you with the flexibility to adapt to whatever sport(s) you eventually play when your body matures.

Change will undoubtedly affect your relationship with sports. You can expect your body and skill level to transform dramatically over your teen years. Most likely you will shed some activities and gain new ones. Be open to this process as the reflection in your mirror changes.

Know Thyself

Although you should *always* seek to learn new skills and grow as a player, it's essential that you know who you are at any point in your development.

Understanding your physical and athletic gifts (or lack of them) is one of the first steps to take in discovering how to play a sport well. By knowing your strengths and weaknesses, you can focus on maximizing the former and minimizing the latter. Through instruction and practices, you can overcome many of your acknowledged weaknesses. And where your physical makeup inherently limits your ability, you can learn how to compensate by adjusting your approach to playing and competing.

With this knowledge of self, you can also concentrate more on playing the positions and team roles best suited to your unique abilities. By doing so, you add value to your team. Your friends will appreciate your willingness to do what's needed to help the team win. Your coach will value your ability to "play within yourself," and likely try to find a role for you on the team.

This self-awareness will also help you find the specific sport(s) in which you can enjoy success at higher levels of play. In more competitive settings, your inherent physical traits, talent, and aptitude are more likely to determine success or failure in certain sports.

So, to improve your ability to play and enjoy sports, you should begin by realistically appraising yourself. Throughout the remainder of this chapter we'll look at some of the key factors you need to consider in your self-analysis.

The Athletic Quality

When someone is successful in sports, we often hear that person referred to as being "athletic." But what does that term mean? What unique characteristics instill this quality in an individual?

The term "athletic" is most often used to describe an individual who has outstanding physical traits (strength, speed, jumping ability). In this context, a person who runs faster and jumps higher is seen as being athletic. For example, the *athletic* figure skater is the one having explosive strength and capable of performing a "quad" jump. Television announcers, when describing a football wide receiver that is big, fast, and can out-jump his defender, will typically comment about the player's outstanding "athleticism."

But what about the quarterback who doesn't run well, but throws a football with incredible accuracy, spin, and speed? What about the basketball player who can't jump high, but has a quick shot release, outstanding range, and accuracy? Similarly, consider the small boy who can somehow shoot (and make) baskets from NBA three point range. The boy's ability is clearly *not* derived from a large body and strong muscles.

Despite lacking ideal physical attributes, these individuals excel through other innate (but less obvious) abilities. Their sports skills are instead supported by extraordinary muscle coordination and visuospatial abilities.

In the case of the small boy described above, a unique mind-body connection exists that enables him to efficiently chain together movements to generate the necessary force to push the ball to the hoop. The football quarterback not only has the same ability (the coordination to throw a hard pass with a tight spiral), but also the visuospatial ability to accurately judge the speed and projected position of a receiver and correspondingly adjust the direction of his pass.

To help you more fully understand the athletic quality, let's revise the traditional definition of athleticism to include these other abilities:

An athletic person is one who possesses *some combination* of the following:

- Outstanding physical characteristics (e.g., speed, strength, quickness, jumping, endurance)

- Exceptional motor skill coordination (control of one's muscle movements)

- Excellent visuospatial abilities (e.g., hand-eye coordination)

When these traits enable an individual to succeed in a sport (and more likely across multiple sports), the person is rightfully stamped "athletic."

Note that an athletic individual can lack one or more of the above components of athleticism. For instance, a successful track and field sprinter may have poor hand-eye coordination. This athlete may not have exceptional motor skill control beyond that necessary to control the various explosive movements related to sprinting.

The point here is to emphasize that athletic excellence in sports is often derived from attributes *other* than the obvious physical ones.

"Athletic" traits besides speed, strength, and jumping ability contribute to an individual's success playing sports. Just because you lack outstanding speed or strength, doesn't mean you aren't an athlete, or that you won't find success playing sports.

The "Athletic" Quality

NOTE: Because the term "athletic" is widely used in its traditional sense (i.e. athletic equals fast, strong, etc.), we chose to use that meaning throughout this book.

The Role of Genetics

Where do the athletic traits we talked about in the prior topic come from? Genetics undoubtedly play a role.

Each of us inherits anatomical features (height, weight, body type) from our parents. Other physical traits, such as strength, speed, and endurance, depend on multiple factors. These include muscle size and composition (fast or slow twitch fibers), lung capacity, and other performance factors such as anaerobic threshold and maximal oxygen uptake. (See the glossary for definitions of these terms.) Scientific research suggests that these factors have a hereditary component—that the capacity to improve one's strength, speed, and endurance via training is dependent on one's genes.

Although your family lineage may place limits on your athletic potential, experts are unsure of how large a role genetics play versus other external factors such as training and diet. Some evidence even suggests that training can affect gene expression (whether the information encoded in a gene ever manifests itself physically). One study found that when people habitually lifted weights, a gene that codes for a muscle-growth-inhibiting protein became less active. [7]

There are also components of the athletic quality, such as balance, agility, reaction time, and hand/eye coordination, that some experts believe are more dependent on training than genetics.

Training for Athleticism

Performance in sports is built upon one's underlying ability to execute fundamental body movements. These movements comprise sports skills such as hitting a baseball, throwing a football, or kicking a soccer ball. They also are the foundation of more general skills such as running, jumping, and cutting. Although possibly constrained by an individual's genetic makeup, the ability to perform these movements responds to training.

You can train your body in a variety of ways. Practicing a sports-specific skill over and over again will help you better execute that skill. It will help you more efficiently chain together the movements that comprise the skill and also help refine any related visuospatial skills. But it doesn't necessarily help improve the underlying physical qualities that support the skill. It doesn't improve the basic physical abilities you need to maximize your success in sports.

To develop these other fundamental qualities, you need to concentrate your training efforts in additional areas.

Most likely, you've already spent a great deal of time developing your ability to run, jump, cut, maintain your balance, and judge the speed and position of moving objects. You've played a lot of childhood games.

The games of "Tag" you played when you were young helped develop your ability to run and quickly change direction. (A "L-cut" in basketball, soccer, or lacrosse is not all that different from the move you used to evade someone trying to touch you in a game of Tag.) Playful wrestling with your brother helped teach you how to keep your center of gravity low and maximize your body leverage—a fundamental physical skill for both a competitive wrestler and a lineman in football. There are many other examples of childhood games that help improve general athleticism. For instance, playing Tetherball, and learning how to strike the ball as it whirls around the pole, helps develop visuospatial recognition and hand/eye coordination. Hopscotch helps improve balance and footwork.

Similar to learning how to play a musical instrument or how to speak another language, it's likely that fundamental athletic skills are best developed at an early age. But these can also be acquired and improved at older ages through training, practice, and play.

As your body matures, dedicated training helps maximize the underlying physical qualities that support your sports skills. You can gain strength by regularly performing calisthenics (sit-ups, pushups) and lifting weights. Plyometric exercises (jump boxes) can improve your jumping ability. Interval training (sprint around three sides of a football field and walk one of the end lines) can improve your cardiovascular endurance.

▶ To improve your athleticism, participate in a wide variety of activities that challenge your mind and body, and provide crossover benefits. For example, juggling and playing table tennis (ping-pong) can help you in sports that require hand-eye coordination.

There are both general and sports-specific training programs that you can try to improve your physical abilities and overall athleticism. Much of the related instruction is available for free on the internet or at your public library. Likewise, commercial DVD's can provide you with comprehensive video instruction.

Today, there are also trainers and clinics that focus solely on the core elements (e.g. strength, speed, agility) associated with improving an athlete's sport performance. Depending on your interest and financial situation, these can both improve your performance and educate you on how best to approach training on your own.

Don't Confuse Athleticism with Talent

Many players, and unfortunately some coaches, look at other players and judge their ability solely based on athleticism—how quickly the players moves, how high they jump, how much they can lift, and how smoothly they execute a sports skill.

Although athleticism is often an essential component of a superior player, the history of amateur and professional sports is full of famous, successful competitors whose physical attributes were far from perfect. Examples include:

- **Larry Bird:** Although he was a great NBA basketball forward who possessed an outstanding outside shot, incredible court sense, and an indomitable will to win, he lacked quickness and jumping ability.

- **Andre Agassi:** One of the best ball strikers of all time, his tennis success was based more on superb hand/eye coordination, exceptional anticipation, and aggressive game tactics than any outstanding physical characteristics.

- **David Ortiz:** Despite being heavy and slow running the base paths, his outstanding ability to hit a baseball has enabled him to enjoy great success and a long career in Major League Baseball.

- **Mike Eruzione:** Considered too small and too slow by professional scouts, he captained the 1980 USA Olympic hockey team, scoring the game winning goal over the heavily favored Soviet Russia team.

At lower levels of competitive play, *many* athletes with limited athleticism are successful. Young athletes with less than ideal body types find ways to win against opponents with more perfect physiques.

Talent is not limited simply to a player's physical characteristics; but also can encompass characteristics more closely associated with the mind and "heart." These less tangible attributes are not as easily seen and measured as the physical ones, but they are important. Performing under pressure, demonstrating character and leadership in difficult moments, persistence, and the will to prepare are all special qualities that can distinguish one athlete from another.

Still another non-athletic talent is an athlete's sports "IQ." An example of this type of intelligence is the ability to understand the time and space relationship between moving objects (ball, players) and correspondingly anticipate opportunities to react before others do. Players with this ability are the ones who always seem to be "around the ball." In basketball, they're the undersized player that "gets yet another rebound." In football, they're the defenders who are "involved in every tackle."

You should also understand that these types of talents are ones that many other players do not inherently possess. Don't underestimate their importance. They can provide you with a competitive advantage against physically superior athletes.

Several years ago, I coached a middle school basketball team that included a seemingly non-athletic eighth grade boy who moved awkwardly, without much speed or quickness. He lacked ball skills and the ability to consistently convert any shot other than a layup. In evaluating John, my first impression was that I would need to find limited roles for him to play. Although having only average height and jumping ability, the forward position was the one best suited to his physical build and abilities.

In our first practices and games, I noticed that John was always around the ball, running the floor, constantly positioning himself to receive passes and rebound the ball. He had an uncanny ability to anticipate ball and player movements, and position himself to gain an advantage.

As John's shot improved through the course of the season, and he learned more individual skills and team concepts, he became one of our team's most valuable players, helping lead us to a victory in our league's championship game.

So even when you don't possess the ideal physical characteristics for your sport, remember that there are still many paths to success.

> ▶ Evaluate yourself and understand what you do better than other players. Make these talents an integral part of how you execute your game.

You're *Not* Too Small, Heavy or Slow

When you look at yourself in the mirror, what do you see? Do you know *who you are?* Many young athletes look at themselves and assume that their body type and other physical attributes will limit their ability to succeed in sports.

But there's a principle called *compensation*—and just as it applies to other aspects of your life, it also applies to sports. *The basic idea is that a physical characteristic that limits you in some way also provides you with an advantage.*

For instance, you may be shorter and heavier than other players on your basketball team. You may find it difficult to defend the lighter, quicker players in open space and you're seemingly too small to rebound against the taller players.

But if you're observant, you will likely notice that your extra weight and low center of gravity provide you with an advantage in certain situations, such as:

- When you set a screen, defenders have a difficult time getting past you; when they make contact, they "bounce" off you.

- When you "post up" a taller, lighter player with good jumping ability, you are able to easily maneuver them with your hip, and gain the position you need close to the basket. You can also easily "seal them out," enabling you to receive a pass and put the ball up for a lay-up.

- Likewise, when you rebound the ball, you notice that you can get the inside position and leverage your low center of gravity and weight to push your more athletic opponent away from the rim—letting the ball come down to a point where *you* can grab the rebound.

▶ Understand the different ways that you can physically succeed within your sport. Small players are often quick; heavy players are usually wide and strong; slow players may have a quick first step (or anticipate well). Know your strengths and use them to your advantage.

Realistically appraise both your strengths and weaknesses—but as previously discussed, also recognize that these qualities may change as you physically mature. Work to improve all parts of your game when you're young. As you develop and mature, you will want to maximize your strengths and minimize the exposure of your weaknesses.

When you get older and the level of competition increases, compensating for your deficiencies becomes more challenging. Physical shortcomings are amplified. Skills that once set you apart from others may now be considered average.

Still, players at the highest levels succeed despite their limitations. And it's not just average professionals who find ways to compensate for their deficiencies—sometimes it's even a sport's "superstar."

Steve Nash, the All-Pro NBA guard, is one such player. By most basketball standards, Steve Nash has outstanding natural attributes and excellent athleticism. At the NBA level, however, he's small and lacks the necessary quickness to defend well. He compensates for these weaknesses with exceptional ball-handling and passing skills (he's ambidextrous), along with an excellent outside shot. Despite his physical limitations, he has twice been selected as the NBA's Most Valuable Player. Even as he approaches the end of his career and age further diminishes his physical abilities, his basketball IQ and unique skills enable him to continue playing at a high level.

There are always exceptions to what the "experts" believe is the required body type needed to excel in a sport. Take for instance the unlikely duo of Nathan Gerbe and Tyler Myers, two hockey players on the Buffalo Sabres 2013 NHL hockey team. Each has discovered how to compete at the highest level despite their unusual stature.

Nathan Gerbe (5'5") and Tyler Myers (6'8") of the Buffalo Sabres NHL hockey team. [JARNO JUUTI/ ILTALEHTI]

Is another sport a better fit?

Also recognize that the principle of compensation applies *across different sports*. A body type or set of physical characteristics may be a weakness in one sport while a strength in another. A tall girl is unlikely to find success in competitive gymnastics, but may excel in volleyball or basketball. A slower, larger boy may struggle in sports that put a premium on speed and quickness, but fare well as a lineman in football where size and strength are important.

The table on the following page provides some examples of "negative" physical traits, compensatory abilities, and related sports that are often a good fit.

Keep an open mind to all of the possibilities; always consider how you can translate a supposed limitation into an advantage. Whether it's a new position, different sport, or adapting your style of play, you have many ways to still achieve success.

The Compensation Principle (examples)

"Negative" physical traits	Compensatory physical abilities	Possible sports (positions)
• Short	• Explosive quickness and strength; fast	• Gymnastics; wrestling; football RB/CB; hockey
• Heavy	• Strong; wide	• Football lineman; shot-put/discus thrower
• Slow	• Good motor skill coordination and visuospatial perception	• Basketball "spot-up" shooter; pitcher; field goal kicker
• Thin	• Tall, good endurance or hand-eye coordination	• Volleyball, basketball forward; cross-country

Believe in Yourself

As you progress through your life in sports, you will likely be told at some point that you're not good enough. It may be others you play with, some of whom will do so with their own interests in mind. These people may see you as competition, and try to undermine your confidence. You may also receive advice that is well-meaning, but nevertheless shortsighted or inaccurate.

If you're fortunate, your friends, family, and coaches will provide ample support and opportunity for you to discover where your talents lie. Try to surround yourself with people who make you better—not those who drag you down.

Remember that playing sports well depends not only on your physical abilities, but also the confidence with which you play. Confidence is earned. A desire to learn, the will to prepare, and hours of practice all increase your ability and value—and in the process, foster your confidence. With added confidence, success appears, and a *virtuous circle* begins. Your successes motivate you to learn and practice more, all of which reinforces your belief in your abilities. A vague whisper within you becomes an ever-present voice that speaks loudly, "I can do this."

Whether it's physical maturation, good genes, talent, applying the compensation principle, or training, you have many possible paths to success in sports. As you consider who and where you are in your personal sports journey, stay positive. Stubbornly seek your own identity and a full understanding of what you're capable of achieving.

What Your Parents Want

I know my parents love me, but sometimes they're very critical about how I played in a game. It just seems that they get carried away about my sports. What can I do?

... Emily

Your journey in sports begins with your parents. When you're young, your parents control your opportunity to participate in sports. Their views on issues related to participation all affect your exposure, access to, and enjoyment of sports. These issues include your safety, the importance of sports relative to other activities (academics), and sometimes the specific sports in which they believe you should participate.

Your parents make choices for you. They set boundaries. They do so with your welfare in mind.

Like you, your parents have hopes and aspirations regarding your time spent in sports. They want to see you succeed in one form or another. Most parents are supportive and show a healthy interest in their child's sports experiences.

But parents aren't perfect. They're not always informed, and consequently may act without fully understanding a situation. Worse yet, some parents can let their own unreasonable passions drive their behavior towards your participation in sports.

This chapter covers some of the sports-related issues you may face with your parents as you mature. When you're older, you may need to step forward and communicate to them how you feel about playing sports.

Parenting Styles

By many accounts, parenting is an art. Parents take different paths in raising their children. Your mom or dad may have an entirely different view on sports than your friend's parents.

Your parents may decide to place you in an organized sports program when you're very young. They may even pay for personalized instruction. If this is the case, your mom and dad probably view organized sports as the best introduction to sports—and the earlier you start the better. They may even believe that organized sports are the *only* venue for you to play sports.

Meanwhile, your friend's mom and dad may place less emphasis on sports. They may view sports as one activity out of several that may potentially become a passion as their child matures. Less concerned with propelling their child into sports at an early age, they apply a broad brush in painting their child's opportunities. To your friend's parents, sports are the games you play on your own with other kids in your neighborhood or at the local community center.

Some parents may place a greater importance on hard work, discipline, and structure; others may instead emphasize creativity, fun, and the curiosity to explore. Your mom or dad may insist that you take piano lessons to both expose and prepare you to enjoy playing music later in life. Meanwhile, your other parent may also recognize your early passion for sports, providing you with a basketball, baseball glove and other equipment so that you can readily explore playing sports. Some parents may ignore your life in sports altogether.

You may not initially enjoy some of the activities your parents push you into. The piano lessons your parents insist you take at first may seem more like work than fun. Your parents may sign you up for a sport you've never played, or put you in a league that includes older kids (playing sports with older players who are better athletes can be a little scary). But these challenges and early learning experiences are essential to your development. Besides providing you with the basic knowledge and skills to participate, they compel you to explore your own unique gifts and begin to understand who you are. And this, in turn, helps prepare you for later success and a deeper enjoyment of life.

Finally, your parents also bring their own set of experiences to their parenting style—including how they were raised. Their attitude toward sports likely reflects their own upbringing.

Whatever your mom and dad's parenting style regarding sports, it initially establishes the context (setting) in which you experience sports.

Your Parents' Safety Concerns

One of your parents' most important concerns, as it relates to your well-being, is your physical safety. There's no getting around this—especially in our wired world where each tragedy involving a child is broadcast 24/7 to every corner of our nation.

Today's parents are sensitized to all of the misfortunes that can possibly befall their child. It doesn't matter whether the risk is statistically real.

Where you live and play affects the potential risks you face. A tough city neighborhood is more dangerous than a gated, suburban community. You need to respect these hazards and your parents' warnings.

There are also real risks associated with playing certain sports. Years ago, parents might worry about their son playing "tackle"

▶ Anytime you step out of your door, there is an increased risk that something can happen to you. Many fun and educational activities include the possibility of personal harm. Mature individuals (including most parents) recognize and manage risks every day. Show your parents that you appreciate their concerns, and tell them the ways in which you are protecting yourself. Be responsible to gain more freedom.

football because he could break his leg. Parents now also worry about their child suffering a head injury that results in a concussion.

Since your parents control your opportunity to play sports, you need to recognize their concerns. And if you independently want to play sports, you will need to come up with ways to dispel your parents' fears.

Listen to your parents' warnings about dealing with strangers and any other potential risks that they believe you may encounter. Respect the boundaries they establish.

As you get older, and your judgment matures, your parents will likely listen to your ideas on managing the risks that concern them. Be proactive about finding win-win solutions. For instance, your local YMCA, community center, or similar facility provides a semi-supervised setting where you and your friends can play. If your parents are reluctant to let you play unsupervised, they may find these facilities an acceptable alternative.

Also consider how you can use technology to alleviate your parents' safety concerns. You have an incredible array of tools available for you to communicate with your parents. Cell phones and smartphones with GPS location-based services provide your parents with a means to stay in touch with you and know where you are. Discuss with your parents how you can possibly use these tools to help satisfy both of your needs.

Some Parents are *Too* Involved

Your parents are an integral part of your journey through youth sports. They provide you with the opportunity to play sports, outfit you with any needed equipment, and offer you their unconditional support. It's the last item—support—that sometimes can cause problems for you.

In their desire to provide their child with the best chance for success, some parents become heavily involved in their child's sports experiences. Many place their child in an organized sports program at an early age. Some sign their child up for multiple sports (in seasons that may overlap each other) trying to provide their child with every possible opportunity. In many cases, family life revolves around scheduled sports activities. Parents attend every game (and many practices). Some parents, especially those who played a sport when they were young, coach their child's youth teams.

All of the above can be good for you—when your parents don't overdo it.

Most of us appreciate the attention and support of our parents. But when your parents actively participate in your sports activities, it can sometimes detract from your unique personal experience in sports.

Your parents' over-involvement can hurt the development of your sense of self-reliance as you become dependent on their support. Instead of dealing with issues on your own, your parents may unnecessarily step in to help. Another potential problem is when your parents push you into multiple youth sports programs or ones that require a huge time commitment. Besides possibly hurting your desire to play sports (burn-out), your life can become scheduled around these programs, limiting your opportunity to explore sports through self-directed, free play (neighborhood pickup games).

Is Your Mom or Dad a "Problem" Sports Parent?

Most parents naturally do a great job shepherding their child through youth sports. But there are many temptations that your parents face that can derail your success in sports. You should recognize some of these more serious parenting issues and how they potentially affect you.

One trap that can snare unsuspecting parents is living vicariously through their child's sports experiences—and basing their own sense of worth on their child's successes or failures. To achieve success, your parents may place an emphasis on the sport that far exceeds your own interest. You, in turn, may develop a distorted perspective of sports, and improperly relate success in sports to your parents' love.

Parents also too often see sports as a vehicle to reach some external reward such as a college scholarship. Despite strong statistics to the contrary, your parents may readily believe that you're on the fast track to a scholarship. Too much emphasis is again placed on sports with the resulting cascade of behaviors that can lead to you eventually quitting sports.

Here are some potentially harmful parental behaviors that your parents should avoid:

- *Defining success only as winning (win/no-win).* Conveying a "Winners win and Losers lose" value may destroy the intrinsic rewards that help drive your long-term participation in sports.

- *Beyond introducing you to a sport, forcing participation.* The goal is for you to find *your* passion—not theirs. This may take you in a direction away from sports and your parents' expectations.

- *Viewing sports as a waste of time with no practical real-world value (and discouraging your participation).* Similar to the above item, a parent's attitudes may neglect your true nature.

- *Becoming too involved in your sports activities (see above).* Whatever the motivation—caring, vicarious enjoyment, parental status—over-involvement can diminish or ruin your independent enjoyment of playing sports.

- *Continually blaming others for your disappointments and setbacks.* Attributing every negative situation to poor coaching or officiating can promote a destructive "victim" mentality in you. (Do your parents constantly yell at the referees and complain about your coach?)

- *Coaching you from the sidelines.* Constant interaction with you during a game can diminish your confidence and self-reliance. Also, coaches dislike this behavior.

Talking with Your Parents

When you're very young, you have little control over your environment. Like most kids, you want to please your parents. But as you get older, you will likely exercise more control over the direction in which your life takes you. You will also naturally become more aware of how your parents' decisions and behavior affect this path.

Regarding your participation in sports, you may begin to notice some of the above problem behaviors in your parents. You may find yourself developing a different view of sports than your parents.

So how can you help them to better understand how you feel about playing sports and why their behavior bothers you?

First, sit down by yourself and try to specifically identify the problem and its cause. Ask yourself questions similar to the ones below:

- Do my parents in some way make me feel uncomfortable around my coach, teammates, friends, or other parents?

- What specific behaviors embarrass me?

- Is my performance somehow suffering because I feel pressured by my parents?

- Do my parents not appreciate how important (or unimportant) sports are to me?

- Am I sure this is about my parents' behavior or is it really some problem that I need to face on my own?

▶ You will need to decide how best to approach your parents. If only one parent's behavior is the problem, then consider talking with your other parent. If one of your parents is more open to listening to you (regardless of who's at fault), then you may want to first speak to that parent. You've faced trouble before with your parents, so you probably know what tactics work best when you need to resolve a problem with them.

This exercise will help you spot the root cause of your discomfort.

Once you identify and feel that you better understand the problem, sit down and talk with one of your parents. Ask them to listen. Depending on your parent's personality, the nature of your relationship with your mom or dad, and how much they've invested emotionally in your sports "career," this conversation may test your courage.

Also appreciate that your parents may not realize how their behavior is affecting you. And without talking to your mom and dad, you may not realize that their *actual* perspective is very different from what you think it is.

Stay True to Yourself

In the end, playing sports is about your fulfillment, enjoyment, and success. It's about *you*—not your mom or dad.

Your parents may expect you to play sports early in your life, signing you up for a youth program whether you like it or not. They may even insist that you practice and accept certain sacrifices. This is not a bad thing when you're young. Many challenges (and changes) occur in your life at that point, and your parents are helping you to overcome fears that will not serve you well later. Also, the skills you learn early on may open the gates to later success and happiness.

But at some point, your destiny in sports becomes your own. If it's different from your parents' expectations, you will need to talk with them. Sports can provide you with many years of fun, fitness, and good friends—but only if you find the path that's true to your own nature.

Fun, Competition, and Community

I've always been real competitive in sports. But sometimes it just doesn't seem fun anymore. Am I missing something?

... Ryan

Your personal journey in sports will wind its way through ups and downs, exhilaration and frustration, and success and failure. You will enjoy moments of elation when you brush perfection. Heartache will sometimes fill your soul when the prize remains out of reach. You will enjoy the camaraderie of playing sports with others, and sometimes face rejection.

Sports, especially in competitive settings, are oppositional in nature. They pit you against an opponent—whether it's a person, a standard of excellence, or your own expectations. This competitive quality can drive our participation.

But besides the thrill of competing, there are a variety of other reasons (positive and negative) why we play sports.

What Leads to a Great Experience Playing Sports?

Central to a positive experience in sports are a set of fundamental elements. These include fun, skill development, heroic moments, increased self-esteem and self-reliance, community, and winning.

Fun

Playing sports provides many rewards—some that are generated internally and others that come from external sources. The most important internal reward for a younger child participating in sports is FUN. It's also important for older, more competitive athletes. As Rafael Nadal, French Open tennis champion once said, "I play because I have fun. If I don't have fun on the court, there is something wrong. I am just a 19-year-old boy that likes to do what he likes, nothing else."

> ▶ Understand that the feeling of "fun" comes in different forms—from the simple joy of running around to more complex variations that embody team play and competition. Depending on your unique personality, choose the sports and competitive level that creates the type of fun *you* find most rewarding!

Besides the immediate gratification of engaging in an enjoyable activity, fun is also *an essential ingredient for long term participation.* Although you may have talent and compete well, the absence of fun will likely lead you to quit when other external rewards (praise, recognition, etc.) are no longer present.

Skill development

Learning and mastering new skills is essential for you to have the necessary tools to participate, contribute, and compete. Although running around and casually playing a sport with your friends may be fun, more rewards and opportunity to play exist when you have mastered fundamental sport skills. One such reward is the self-confidence that is gained from an understanding of how to play a game and do it well.

Heroic moments (and glorious defeats)

Sports are attractive partly because of the various feelings they evoke. Besides fun, there is also the "thrill of victory" and the "agony of defeat." Heroic moments and glorious defeats are an essential part of the sports experience. They come together as a package deal—you can't have one without the other. They impart upon you the potentially lifelong satisfaction of rising up to meet a challenge, and sometimes the heartfelt disappointment of a failed opportunity. Either way, these emotions add depth to your life experience.

Self-esteem and self-reliance

As you learn new skills, gain experience, and progress toward a clearer understanding of how to play a sport, your confidence will naturally grow. This, in turn, leads to an increased sense of self-esteem (satisfaction in oneself). You become more self-reliant, understanding that you individually command tools that can affect the outcome of a game. Your self-reliance also increases as you begin to organize and manage your *own* pickup games (a skill not cultivated within the adult-run games typical of youth leagues).

Community

When you play a sport, you share with other participants the game and its values. This is most evident in team sports, where success is dependent upon the contributions of each team member. But individual sports also provide a sense of community. Shared values are present in all sports.

Community is also present in the bond that ties together athletes of all ages and generations. You and other young athletes feel the same joy and appreciation for sports that your parents, grandparents, and coaches experienced when they were young. You can also

195

play certain sports (golf, tennis, etc.) with family and friends throughout your life.

Winning

And finally, winning is part of a successful sports experience. Viewed with proper perspective, winning is an essential and required reward for continued participation. Everyone likes to experience their fair share of games where the final score favors them. At the most competitive levels, winning on the scoreboard plays a far greater role in defining "success."

But there *are* different ways to define "winning"—especially when you're younger. Consider again the benefits described above. Those glorious defeats, where an individual or team competes courageously against a vastly superior team, do mean something. Improving one's individual performance, regardless of others' performance, is a "win." Learning how to master new skills and successfully interact with others rewards you with the valuable prizes of self-reliance and confidence. And when it comes to winning the battle of lifelong participation and fitness, these other types of victories are often the ones that matter.

💣 Vince Lombardi, a hall of fame NFL coach, once said, "Winning isn't everything. It's the only thing." Although this may be true at the most competitive level of sports, it's *not* true in youth and scholastic sports.

Balancing Internal and External Rewards

As discussed above, a great experience playing sports embodies a set of rewards that drives your desire to play. These rewards come in different flavors.

Internal rewards are ones that are intrinsic to the activity itself—the feelings within you that are evoked when you engage in a certain behavior. These feelings include:

- Satisfaction (from mastering a new skill or performing to personal expectations)

- Excitement (the thrill of participating in a close contest)

- Joy (from running around and releasing physical energy)

- Sense of belonging (to a larger group who share similar values)

- Flow (while playing, experiencing effortless, energized concentration as each moment unfolds)

External rewards, on the other hand, are ones that either come from an outside source (usually another person) or are secondary to the play itself. These external rewards can be either abstract or concrete. For example, praise that you receive from a parent or coach for performing a task well is an *abstract* external reward, as is winning on the scoreboard. When you were young, and your parents treated you to an ice cream cone after a good game, they were reinforcing your enjoyment of the sports experience with a *concrete* external reward.

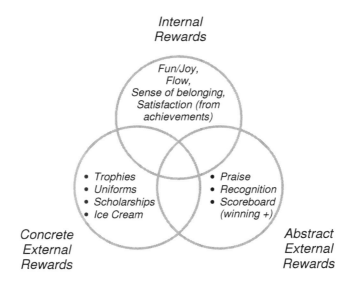

Both internal and external rewards play a role in motivating an athlete. At more competitive levels of play, external rewards such as playing time, public and peer recognition, scholarship offers, and money all can drive your training and performance to higher levels.

But external rewards also have a downside. Too much emphasis on these types of rewards may cause you to lose sight of the intrinsic motivators associated with playing sports. And when the external rewards disappear, so will your desire to participate.

Sometimes the Reward *Is* in Playing Your Best

There are times in sport when the reward of participating in a hard fought contest goes well beyond who wins or loses. The prize won is a deep sense of personal fulfillment based on the knowledge that you prepared and played to the best of your ability.

I learned this lesson at an early age when I played my good friend (also named Jeff) for our town's youth badminton championship. In our age group, Jeff was probably the town's best athlete, talented in all sports. Although not as athletic or physically mature as Jeff, my ability was close to his.

Our match that day was well-played from the beginning. Each point was closely contested, the outcome rarely decided by an unforced error. As the match progressed, the quality of our play only seemed to improve. We each ran down the other's shots, making one outstanding save after another.

Jeff won the first game and I captured the second. In the deciding game, every point became a protracted battle. Each of us took our winning turn. But unfortunately for me, Jeff made

Jeff Abell, Jack Hesslink, me

199

one or two better plays to claim the championship.

As the town's recreation supervisor presented us with our trophies, he told us that he had never seen a better competition at our age. Both Jeff and I already knew how well we had played—and how each of us had brought out the best in the other. Even years later, we occasionally made reference to that special, fulfilling moment when we were young boys.

Striking to win *is* important—it's the ultimate real world measure of your preparation and play. At the highest, most competitive levels of play, it's often the most important reward.

> ● If you only equate success in sports to winning, and base your self-esteem on this value, you will sacrifice the greater rewards that come from playing sports.

But if you see winning and losing only in absolute terms, and not also about you and your team's quality of play and effort, you will lose out on countless moments of joy that sports can provide.

Everybody likes to win, and you should try your best to achieve this result. But sometimes being part of a great contest, or performing to the best of your abilities, is deeply satisfying in and of itself.

More on Community...

Playing sports provides you with many benefits including fun, physical exercise, competition, and an outlet to express yourself. When you get together with your friends in the backyard or driveway for a pickup game, you probably also enjoy the camaraderie—the warm feeling of good fellowship we get when we share an experience with others. To varying degrees, most of us take pleasure in this sense of community.

In both individual and team sports, pickup or organized, you will find many opportunities to be part of an enjoyable shared experience. In some cases you will find others that share the same passion for your sport—who enjoy its beauty and flow, competing to win, or the challenge of testing one's abilities against personal limits or some standard of performance. With these individuals you often find friendship based on this common bond. In other instances, casual or less skilled players may have a limited interest in playing, but do so mainly because they enjoy being part of a group.

In team sports, your teammates share the experience with you. In games with your friends, everybody enjoys the shared friendly competition. Even in more serious competitive situations, with opponents you do not know, there is often a mutual respect based on everyone's shared passion and enjoyment of the sport. You and your opponent are both part of the same community.

Individual sports also provide an opportunity for community—each competitor respectful of the other's similar passion and commitment. Individual competitors can even find a sense of team between each other in certain situations. For example, two competitive tennis players representing rival schools may find themselves supporting and rooting for each other in a distant tournament.

As you grow older, and begin to experience more injuries or responsibilities that take you away from your game, you will come to value the communal aspect of sports even more. In your pursuit of excellence, always try to respect your teammates, opponents and the game itself. Recognize and appreciate that you are all part of the same community, and that your sport makes the reward of this shared experience possible.

▶ In team sports, try to minimize internal cliques (i.e., small groups) and their often destructive effect on the chemistry of your team. Find and promote shared common ground with all of your teammates. If you're in a position to lead, try to recognize potential disruptions within your team before they grow and take hold. A key word from you to another player may be all that's needed to short-circuit a potential problem.

Be a Leader—Help Your Less-Talented Teammates Succeed

The success of your team is based not only on how well you play, but also on how well your teammates play. Although *you* may perform at a high level, possibly to the best of your ability, do you also help your teammates reach their potential?

If you're one of the more talented or experienced players on your team, you're likely in a position to exercise team leadership. One way to lead is to do so by example. If a talented player demonstrates a positive attitude and work ethic, other players will tend to follow this example. Some players will also watch how you play and naturally pick up on some of your skills and techniques.

> ▶ Like a good coach, you need to understand how to best communicate information to your teammates. Pick key moments, provide constructive comments and direction, reinforce positive plays by your lesser skilled teammates, and avoid negative comments. Hand out praise ("Nice pass/shot," etc.) Above all—communicate!

Beyond setting an example, what else can you do? As a player, you have a unique advantage over your coach—you're out there on the court or field interacting with your teammates during each moment of the game. You have the opportunity to advise and "teach" your lesser skilled teammates as game events occur.

You may find some players very open to learning from you. Take a few minutes before or after practice and help these teammates improve a skill or correct a bad habit.

Besides helping your teammates improve as players, there's another important area in which your leadership can make a difference. In neighborhood games, locker rooms, and other group situations, you will sometimes witness a weaker boy (or girl) become the subject of another kid's poor joke, intimidation, hazing or other demeaning behavior. It's easy to sit back, not risk your standing within the group, and let events like this unfold to their unfortunate conclusion. It's also an opportunity, however, for you to demonstrate one of the more noble aspects of superior leadership—that the strong help the weak. Speak up and tell others to knock it off.

If you've ever been picked on and had someone else come to your defense, you know how you felt afterwards toward your protector. He or she earned your admiration and loyalty. Not only is defending others in these situations the right thing to do, but it also can boost your standing among your peers. Everyone respects the person who stands up to the bully or "mean girl."

Rise above your own individual game and comfort zone and help your teammates whenever possible. In addition to benefiting your own self-interest by improving your team, you will find that your leadership efforts also reward you with a sense of satisfaction in helping others achieve.

Down the Road

Throughout this book, I've discussed the many excellent benefits that sports can bring to you. When you're young, sports are mainly about having fun, finding success, fitting in, and enjoying the shared experience of playing sports with other like-minded kids. That's as it should be.

Playing sports in your youth also provides potential benefits for you later in life. Good health, the learning of important life skills, and a stronger sense of community head the list of benefits that can accrue to the adult who participated in a positive sports experience as a child.

The aging process inevitably erodes our physical abilities. For the professional athlete, this happens at a relatively early age. But for those who play and compete at a lesser level, recreational sports can provide a lifetime of benefits.

Although family, work and other adult responsibilities may make finding the time to play sports more challenging, there is no inherent reason why anyone without a serious health condition needs to stop playing. Yes, your sports activities will evolve. You'll drop some sports you enjoyed in your youth and probably add new ones.

But if you enjoy sports for the right reasons now, it's likely you will still enjoy them later in life. Some things don't necessarily change as we age. Few older people would disagree with the following humorous observation:

"Age does not diminish the extreme disappointment of having a scoop of ice cream fall from the cone." (Jim Fieberg)

So if you like sports, consider how the choices of your youth can affect your opportunity to enjoy playing sports later in life.

Play multiple sports

As already discussed earlier in this book, there are many reasons why playing multiple sports when you're young is preferable to specializing in a single sport. In addition to causing burnout and overuse injuries, focusing too early on a single sport removes potential crossover benefits from other sports. Early specialization also removes the opportunity for you to experience other sports that may be a better fit when your body and mind matures.

But specialization also has negative *long-term* effects.

First, it reduces the opportunity for you to enjoy a wider range of great youth sports experiences—the ones that create memorable, satisfying moments. Limiting yourself to a single sport can also decrease your opportunity to meet new friends. These other kids may be very different from those who participate in your main sport. These friendships can enrich your life.

By playing multiple sports, you provide a solid foundation for a lifetime of sports participation. Developing a well-rounded set of athletic skills and knowledge enables you to more easily adapt to whatever adult sports activity interests you later in life.

Life-Long Sports

At some point during your youth, you'll probably play some tennis, table tennis (ping-pong), badminton, or other racquet sport. You may pick up your dad's seven iron and hit a Whiffle golf ball around your yard. Maybe you'll make it out to a real golf course and play eighteen holes.

Although you and your friends may not regularly play these sports, they're still fun. And unlike some of the other sports you play in your youth, these ones may play a larger role in your adult life.

Keep in mind that certain sports are simply more conducive to adult participation—either from the physical aspect or their availability.

Adults can play racquet sports (tennis, platform tennis, racquetball) and golf throughout most of their lifetime. These sports are less taxing on your body than sports such as football, rugby, soccer, or competitive basketball. This is important as you age and your body becomes more easily injured.

Availability is another important factor in whether you continue to play sports as an adult. Although you may find pickup games of touch football in your twenties or thirties, this is less likely in middle age and later. Meanwhile, pickup basketball games (half or full court) are readily available at your local YMCA or other public facility for adults of all ages. Softball and co-ed volleyball leagues are plentiful.

By playing these other sports, you are laying the foundation to enjoy sports throughout your lifetime. Having been exposed to a sport early in life and developing some basic skills, you can easily come back to the sport later in life. You can walk into a situation and immediately show that you know the game and have at least some skill. All of which makes it more likely that you will continue to play sports as an adult and reap the benefits (fun, good health, etc.) of doing so!

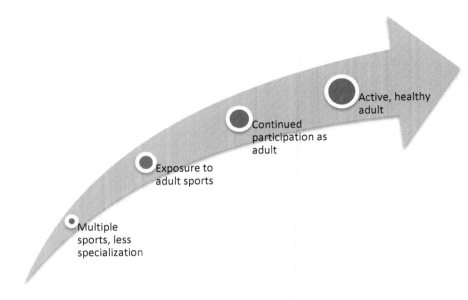

Active, healthy adult

Continued participation as adult

Exposure to adult sports

Multiple sports, less specialization

Competing in Life

Sports competition is little different from other competitive situations that you will face early in your life, including:

- Earning academic achievements (honor roll, National Honor Society)

- Earning college scholarship money (academic)

- Gaining entrance to your preferred college

- Getting your first job

Sports can provide you with an understanding of what competition means. You learn that one's natural talent is often secondary to hard work and dedication. You learn what success and failure feel like—and how to steer toward success and away from failure. And you learn how to balance your individual needs with those of others to achieve success that benefits everyone.

Liking What You See in the Rear View Mirror

As you progress through life, you will encounter many challenges—ones that you rise to meet and others where you fall short. Both your successes and failures impart wisdom. Sometimes they place an indelible mark on your sense of self.

Risking failure is necessary to achieve great success. Failing to convert a game winning shot always hurts; you will remember that moment for a long time (if not the rest of your life). But if you tried and gave it your best effort, you will also likely be at peace with yourself.

Failure stings all the more when you're unable to face a difficult moment. The regret that fills you is not easily erased, and is usually more painful in the long run than simply confronting your fear and taking whatever lumps come your way.

Your successes, on the other hand, can impart to you a long-lasting sense of pride and satisfaction. No one can ever take away from you that special moment when you conquered some difficult challenge—whether it's a talented foe or the seemingly unsurpassable limits of your personal abilities. The shot you make at the end of the game, the unlikely victory over a superior opponent, unexpected moments of athletic perfection, and knowing you played to the best of your ability in a losing contest, are all examples of this type of success.

In sports, like other parts of your life, walk a path that you're satisfied with when you look back. Know that you were open to experiencing new opportunities. Have stories to tell. Be content that you prepared and gave your best effort when you confronted some challenge. Have fun.

Enjoy your journey through sports and life!

Acknowledgements

My youth was filled with countless hours of joy, much of it rooted in sports. Whether playing a backyard game of touch football with friends, practicing free throws on a neighbor's rim, or competing in organized sports, there seemed to me so many different ways to enjoy playing sports.

Many of my current friends and associates experienced sports in the same way. Some have helped me refine the advice presented in this book. I would especially like to thank Diane Krill, Jeff Lampo, Stan Blaylock, Paul Evans, Norm Mast, Kevin Holleran, and Jack Connors for their help in reviewing this material and making suggestions for its improvement. A special thanks to Mary Jane Williams for copyediting the final text. Also, thanks to Michael Brocks, David Littlefield, and Bud Bailey for their review of an earlier manuscript that contained some of the material presented here.

Leaning on one's experience to find essential truths is only part of composing relevant counsel for others; validating that one's ideas still apply is also necessary. To this end, I want to thank some of my younger contributors, including Michael Spence, Luke Brocks, Sierra Perlick, Davis Blaylock, and Kyle Taylor for their unique perspective and advice.

I'm also grateful to all those who helped create my own joyful experience playing sports when I was young. From the kids of Boncrest to the parents who supported our opportunity to play, each helped make my journey in sports a more rewarding one. (Thanks Mrs. Syrcher for turning on the spotlight so I could shoot hoops in your driveway after dark!)

As always, I would like to thank my parents, teachers and coaches who were supportive through both my successes and failures. A special thanks to my elementary school gym teacher, Jack Hesslink, who early on appreciated and helped foster my love for playing sports. And to John Cashmore, one of my youth football coaches: Thanks for taking the blame on calling a pass play at the one yard line of our opponent—after I threw an interception. The little things do matter.

Appendix:
Sports Terms

This appendix contains an alphabetical listing of various sports and scientific terms used in this book. Italicized words in a term's explanation are defined elsewhere in this glossary. Many of the scientific term's explanations are paraphrased from related articles contained in *Wikipedia, The Free Encyclopedia.* You can go online to learn more.

Aerobic As related to exercise, muscular energy that is derived from oxygen supplied by the heart and lungs. An example of aerobic exercise is walking or bicycling.

Anaerobic As related to exercise, muscular energy derived from stored substances (Glycogen carbohydrates) as opposed to oxygen (Aerobic). An example of anaerobic exercise is strength training.

Anaerobic Threshold (also Lactate Threshold) The point at which lactate (a byproduct of muscular exertion) is produced faster than it can be removed. Muscular contraction is eventually impaired; normal symptoms include muscle fatigue, ache and a burning sensation. This threshold varies among individuals and can be increased with training. *Interval training* takes advantage of the body being able to temporarily exceed the lactate threshold, and then recover (reduce blood-lactate) while operating below the threshold and while still doing physical activity.

Athletic Position A body position that enables effective movement. Sometimes referred to as the *Ready* start-up position; but, more generally, can also refer to a body position during movement. Typified by bent knees, proper footwork, and balance control.

Athletic Scholarship An award of financial aid to an individual to attend a college or university, based predominantly on his or her ability to play a sport.

Athleticism A quality of an athlete that typically refers to the athlete's natural physical traits (strength, speed, jumping ability). In this context, a person who runs faster and jumps higher is seen as being athletic. In a broader context, the term can also apply to an athlete who may lack one or more of the aforementioned physical characteristics, but demonstrates excellent *motor skill* coordination and *visuospatial* skills (e.g. the football quarterback who isn't fast but has excellent arm strength and accurately throws a tightly spiraled pass).

Backdoor A common play used in many team sports where an offensive player slips behind a defender to receive a pass. Typically used against an aggressive defender who is preventing a direct pass and/or is looking toward the ball or puck (and not the player defended).

Blocking Out *See* Boxing Out

Boxing Out A basketball technique in which one player gains inside position and uses his or her body to obstruct an opponent from getting a rebound or tipping in a shot. Also referred to as "blocking out," this general technique of positioning oneself between an opponent and the goal is also used in other sports including hockey and lacrosse.

Burnout A psychological term for exhaustion and diminished interest. In sports, burnout can result from overtraining, specializing in a single sport, and an overemphasis on external rewards (winning, awards) vs. internal intrinsic ones (fun).

Center of Gravity (COG) The imaginary point around which a body can be balanced. A person's COG is typically located near the belly button, but it varies depending on body type and position. (It can be outside the body as when a high jumper bends to clear the bar.) A COG that is inside its base of support (e.g. wide athletic stance) is stable whereas a position outside its base (e.g. narrow athletic stance) is not.

Competitive Advantage In sports, some combination of athletic traits, skills, playing conditions or knowledge that provides you with an edge while competing against an opponent.

Cut A type of player movement used to gain separation from a defender, usually characterized by an abrupt acceleration away from the player's current position to a new one. An example is a "V-cut" where a player plants his or her lead foot and then changes direction at an extreme sharp angle.

Cross-Training A training technique that involves exercising your body using different activities (ones that engage different muscle groups). Cross-training can both improve your general fitness and protect against overuse injuries. Also, playing one sport can sometimes help improve a specific skill in another sport.

External Rewards Ones that come from an outside source and are extrinsic to the play itself (e.g., awards, trophies). *See also* Internal Rewards

Fast/Slow Twitch The two primary types of muscle fibers comprising skeletal muscles. Fast twitch fibers fire more quickly than slow twitch fibers, and are better at producing short bursts of energy. Slow twitch fibers contract more slowly but can generate continuous muscle contractions over an extended period. Each person's mixture of these two muscle fiber types is genetically determined. Sprinters typically have a greater number of fast twitch fibers while marathon runners would conversely have more slow twitch fibers.

Gamesmanship Player behaviors (psychological tricks, "trash talking," and physical intimidation) intended to undermine an opponent's capacity to compete.

Give and Go A common two-man play used in many team sports where an offensive player first passes to a teammate and then *cuts* toward the goal to receive a return pass.

Hand-eye Coordination The coordinated control of vision and hand movements to perform a task. *See also* Visuospatial

Intangibles Less obvious, non-athletic qualities that help athletes achieve success playing sports. These include attitude, willingness to learn and prepare, attention to detail, the ability to perform at a high level in pressure situations (a "clutch" player), never giving up ("heart"), and leadership.

Internal Rewards Ones intrinsic to the sports activity itself (e.g., fun, satisfaction). *See also* External Rewards

Interval Training A cardiovascular training technique that involves bursts of high intensity effort intermixed with short periods of recovery. The high intensity "intervals" are usually near 100% effort. For example, an athlete who repeatedly sprints around three sides of soccer field and jogs one of the end lines is using interval training.

Kinesthesia (adj. **Kinesthetic**) A perceptive sense used to determine the relative position of one's body parts. This occurs through a feedback mechanism that involves the tension and contraction of muscles. Kinesthesia is a key component of *muscle memory* and *hand-eye coordination*. An example is when you close your eyes and touch your hands to your nose.

Man-to-Man A type of defense in which each player is assigned to guard and follow the movements of a single offensive player.

Maximal Oxygen Uptake (VO₂ max) The maximum volume of oxygen that a person can use in one minute of intense exercise; a measure that reflects the physical fitness of an individual.

Muscle Memory A form of memory that allows one to perform a physical task without conscious effort. It's typically developed through the repetition of a movement many times.

Mental Mistake A mistake of commission or omission—one that typically results from poor judgment or lack of attention. (As opposed to *physical* mistakes of commission that result from the failure to properly execute a sports skill).

Motor Skill A learned sequence of movements that combine to produce a smooth, efficient action in order to perform a task.

Nautilus Machine A type of equipment commonly used in strength training.

Off-the-Ball A term used to refer to game action occurring away from the ball.

Organized Sports A form of sports play organized and run by parents or other adults. Little League Baseball is an example of an organized youth sports program.

Peripheral Vision The part of one's visual field that occurs outside the very center, and extends to its outermost edges. Used by athletes to recognize motion at the edges of their field of view.

Pick A blocking move where an offensive player moves to a stationary position next to a defender, blocking the defender from following the offensive player he or she is guarding. Also referred to as a *Screen*. Extensions of the simple Pick include the Pick-and-Roll and the Pick-and-Pop.

Pick-and-Roll A two-man play in which the player who sets a pick then pivots and moves ("rolls") toward the goal looking for a return pass.

Pick-and-Pop A two-man play in which the player who sets a pick then moves ("pops") away from the goal looking for a return pass.

Pickup A form of sports play organized and run by the players themselves. Pickup games refer to those played among neighborhood friends and more competitive ones played at a park, community center, or school.

Pitch Count The number of pitches thrown by a pitcher in a game.

Playing Down When a person plays sports with younger or less-skilled players for the purpose of relaxation, fun, reversing *burn-out*, or learning how to play a more central *team role* (e.g. "scorer").

Playing Up When a person plays sports with older or more skilled players for the purpose of developing and testing new skills, or learning how to play more supportive *team roles* ("defender," "passer").

Ready Position An *athletic position* of "readiness" that enables quick movement in any direction from a stationary startup position. Typified by feet spread, knees bent, head up, arms at side with hands at hip level and palms turned inward.

Screen A blocking move where an offensive player moves to a stationary position next to a defender, blocking ("screening") the defender from following the offensive player he or she is guarding. Used in team sports such as basketball and lacrosse, and sometimes (illegally) in other sports such as football. Also known as a *Pick*.

Service Line In racquet sports, the back line of the service box (the area in which the served ball must hit).

Showcase Camp A type of sports camp attended by college recruiters that gives prospective students an opportunity to display ("showcase") their abilities.

Small-Sided Games Ones with teams that are comprised of a smaller number of players than required in an official game. Neighborhood games, such as 2-on-2 pickup basketball, are an example.

Sports IQ (Sports Intelligence Quotient) A slang term used in describing an athlete's ability to read and react to situations during play.

Sportsmanship An approach to playing sports rooted in fair play and respect for all elements of the game (rules, opponents, officials).

Star The outstanding player(s) on a team or in a sport.

Stickball A street game related to baseball, usually formed as a pickup game and often associated with play in cities. The equipment consists of a broom handle and a rubber or tennis ball.

Strong-side *See* Weak-side

Switch A man-to-man defensive tactic where two defenders switch the players they are covering. This typically occurs when an offensive player sets a screen for his or her teammate.

Tactics Any skillful method to gain an end. For example, if a team's defensive strategy is to pressure their opponent, supportive tactics might include defenders guarding each opponent closely, double-teaming the ball when possible, and denying passing lanes.

Team Role The part one plays on his or her team. Roles are often defined as either functional ("scorer") or positional ("point guard").

Trash Talk A form of gamesmanship employing comments (often derogatory) intended to affect an opponent's state of mind, disrupting that player's concentration.

Travel Team A team that "travels" to play other teams of similar ability. Especially at the youth sports level, these teams are often comprised of an organization's better players.

Visuospatial The perception of the spatial relationships among objects within the field of vision.

Weak-side The side of the court or field which is away from the ball. Conversely, the strong-side is the side where the ball is located. Each side is established by an imaginary centerline that runs the length of the field and intersects the goals.

Whiffleball A variation of baseball designed for indoor or outdoor play in confined areas. The game is played using a perforated, lightweight, plastic ball and a long, plastic (typically yellow) bat.

Winner A shot that wins a point—often used in tennis and other racquet sports to describe a winning point.

Zone A type of defense in which a player defends an area on the playing field or court (as opposed to a specific opponent).

Notes

[1] Mariane Torbert, *Secrets to Success in Sport & Play* [Prentice-Hall, 1982], 21

[2] Jeffrey M. Willardson, "Core Stability Training: Applications to Sports Conditioning Programs," *Journal of Strength and Conditioning Research* (2007, 21(3), 979-985)

[3] Dejan Kovacevic, "Retooled Morton on the rise," *Pittsburgh Post Gazette* (May 3, 2011)

[4] Brad Gilbert and Steve Jamison, *Winning Ugly* [Fireside, 1994], 226

[5] Earnest L. Thayer, "Casey at the Bat," *The Examiner* (June 3, 1888)

[6] Andrew Hill, *Be Quick—But Don't Hurry* [Simon & Shuster, 2001], 147

[7] David Epstein, "Sports Genes," *Sports Illustrated* (May 17, 2010)

Index

Index

overuse, 60, 151
R.I.C.E, 24
intangibles, 141, 156
interval training. *See* conditioning
Jackson, Phil, 105
Johnson, Earvin "Magic", 138
Jordan, Michael, 135–36
juggling, 176
jump boxes, 176
Kansas, University of, 126
Kapono, Jason, 167
kickball, 165
kinesthesia, 7
lacrosse, 93, 145
  backdoor play, 96
leadership, 29, 178
  and character, 156–57
  bullying, stopping, 203
  helping teammates, 202–3
learning
  breaking down skills, 46–48
  correcting deficiencies in the
    offseason, 51–55
  formal and informal, 33–34
  imagination and, 51
  in sports, 35
  know your strengths and
    weaknesses, 171–72
  outside of comfort zone, 50
  overexaggerate technique, 55–57
  resources, 44–46
life-long sports
  benefits of, 204
  playing multiple sports in youth,
    204
limitations, knowing, 78
Lincoln, Abraham, 169
Lombardi, Vince, 196
Los Angeles Lakers, 105
Manning, Peyton, 86
man-to-man. *See* defense, man-to-man
maximal oxygen uptake, 175
McEnroe, John, 129
mini-games, 101
mistakes
  mental, 153
  minimizing, 154
  physical, 153
Morton, Charlie, 56
movement
  fundamentals of, 1–6

without the ball, 154–55
multiple sports
  benefits of playing, 59–61
  coaches view of, 60
  complementary, 151
  selecting, 61, 181
  skill crossover, 59
muscle memory, 49, 58
muscles
  fast and slow twitch fibers, 174
Myers, Tyler, 181
Nadal, Rafael, 194
Nash, Steve, 180
NBA, 90, 105, 135, 167, 177, 180
New York Yankees, 127
NFL, 88, 168, 196
Nike, 16, 136
nutrition, 21–22
  60/20/20 rule, 21
  dehydration, 21
  fluid replacement drinks, 22
  postgame, 22
  pregame meal, 21
  supplements, 22
  websites, 22
off-ball opportunities, 95–98
organized sports
  benfits of playing, 37–38
  downside of playing, 38–39
Ortiz, David, 177
Owens, Jessie, 138
parents
  different parenting styles, 186–87
  problem behaviors, 189–91
  safety concerns, 187–88
  talking with, 191–92
  who are too involved, 188–89
patterns of play, 90, 91, 101, *See also*
    three-man play patterns, *See also*
    two-man play patterns
peripheral vision, 7
persistence, 178
Phillips, Wade, 88
pick. *See* Screen
pick-and-pop. *See* two-man play
    patterns
pick-and-roll. *See* two-man play
    patterns
pickup games, 65–80
  1-2-3 Shoot!, 72
  arguments, dealing with, 73

Index

The Joy of Youth Sports: Creating the Best Youth Sports Experience for Your Child

For the parent who is looking to discover how his or her child can enjoy success in sports, *The Joy of Youth Sports* is your essential guide. This book describes five steps to a great youth sports experience—the one that not only maximizes athletic abilities, but also helps a child develop life skills and a joyful appreciation for playing sports.

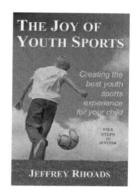

Whether you're a parent, coach, or both, this book will also help you understand the role you play in creating a successful, rewarding youth sports experience.

Sports parents will discover:
- The best ways to support your child
- Behavioral traps to avoid
- How to evaluate a coach

Parent coaches will:
- Learn positive coaching techniques
- Gain insight on how to evaluate players
- Discover how to use team roles to help each child find success

For more information on how to enjoy
a great youth sports experience, visit:

WWW.INSIDEYOUTHSPORTS.ORG

35375995R00142

Made in the USA
Lexington, KY
09 September 2014